A YEAR IN CHINA

A YEAR IN CHINA

Jon Perrywell and Vincent Sack

MILTON KEYNES ● COLORADO SPRINGS
● HYDERABAD

14 13 12 11 10 09 08   8 7 6 5 4 3 2 1

This edition published 2008 by Authentic Media
9 Holdom Avenue, Bletchley, Milton Keynes, MK1 1QR, UK
1820 Jet Stream Drive, Colorado Springs, CO 80921, USA
OM Authentic Media, Medchal Road, Jeedimetla Village,
Secunderabad 500 055, A.P., India
www.authenticmedia.co.uk

Authentic Media is a division of IBS-STL U.K., limited by guarantee, with its
Registered Office at Kingstown Broadway, Carlisle, Cumbria CA3 0HA.
Registered in England & Wales No. 1216232. Registered charity 270162

British Library Cataloguing in Publication Data
A catalogue record for this book is available from the British Library

ISBN-13: 978-1-85078-815-7

Cover Design by fourninezero design.
Print Management by Adare
Printed in Great Britain by J.H. Haynes & Co., Sparkford

OMF International works throughout East Asia, as well as seeking to reach East Asians all over the world. OMF was founded by James Hudson Taylor in 1865 as the China Inland Mission. Their 1200 workers are committed to glorifying God through the urgent evangelization of East Asia's billions; sharing the gospel, planting churches, teaching the Bible, helping the needy and working in partnership with East Asia's church.

OMF also places Christians with professional skills and a dedication to bringing their witness to their workplace in a wide range of educational, social and development roles throughout China and East Asia.

In line with this, OMF Publishing seeks to motivate and equip Christians to make disciples of all peoples. Publications cover:

- Stories and biographies showing God at work in East Asia;
- The biblical basis of mission and mission issues;
- The growth and development of the church in Asia;
- Asian culture and religion.

Books, booklets, articles and free downloads can be found on our website at www.omf.org. Addresses for OMF's English-speaking centres can be found at the back of this book.

Character List

Ping Chang A first year student studying English at Shencheng Agricultural University. She is originally from a peasant family.

Mrs Chang Ping Chang's mother. A peasant woman. Her husband has gone to find manual work in the city, leaving Mrs Chang at home with her three children: Ping, and the twins, Han and Feng.

Xiao Han Ping Chang's younger brother (Xiao being a term of endearment). Han becomes unwell while Ping is at university.

Xiao Feng Ping Chang's younger brother (Xiao being a term of endearment).

Beng Chu A second-year student studying English at the university. The son of wealthy parents who are members of the Communist Party.

Mr and Mrs Chu Beng Chu's mother and father. They are wealthy and well connected, with great expectations of their son.

Zhao Ping Chang's friend. She is from a relatively well-off family.

Mei Li A student at the university, one of Jon's students who attends the Bible studies he runs.

Wang Dan   A final-year student at the university, from a poor, rural family. He is in a relationship with Lin Yang.

Lin Yang   A student at the university, from a well-off family. Lin is in a relationship with Wang Dan though her father disapproves of his poor background.

Mr Yang   Lin's father. His wife is dead.

Mr Luo   The sports coach at the university. Though married, he has an affair with Mei Li, his student.

Shen   Jon's friend from Shencheng and a new Christian. He goes to work in Beijing but has difficulties with his employers.

Hui and Lian   Two Chinese Christian students at the university. They help Jon and Simon by translating during Bible studies.

Yin Hong   A student at the university, he is from a wealthy family that is well connected within the Communist Party. He is a 'little emperor' who gets by on connections alone.

Jon Perrywell   A British teacher at the university. Jon is on a year's placement in Shencheng.

Simon   A Scottish teacher living in Shencheng. He shares a flat with Jon and is involved in similar outreach. Simon is also in Shencheng for one year.

Charlotte   A British teacher living in Shencheng and working alongside Jon and Simon. Charlotte is also in Shencheng for one year.

Matthew and Sarah   A British couple living in Shencheng long-term. They work in the English training centre and are involved with outreach alongside Jon, Simon and Charlotte.

1.

The journey had been hot and long. At the train station in the city centre she was jostled along as the vast crowd was compressed into a single file and fed through the final ticket gate. The concourse spread out before Ping and she stood overwhelmed by the sight: people standing, squatting and even sleeping while they waited for trains, hordes milling around looking for taxis or buses. She found herself swept along with the tide of people. Shoved from side to side, she struggled to move forward with her huge bag towards the bus. It took her several attempts to get on board but eventually Ping found herself sandwiched in the middle of a mass of bodies in the centre aisle of the bus, with her arms pinned to her sides, just about managing to keep hold of her bag. At all costs she couldn't let go – thieves abounded at stations looking for rich pickings among the travellers.

Oddly, for the first part of the bus ride she felt protected, despite the constant swaying and frequent lurching stops. Only those nearest the sides and back of the bus suffered from being thrown against hard seat backs or windows. Hemmed in as she was she rocked against the bodies around her. For some time she saw nothing of Shencheng city but could only look at the head and shoulders of the other people. They snatched furtive glances, sizing up each person that they were forced to travel with. She had ended up wedged behind a man wearing a traditional Mao suit, still the normal dress of the older generation of Chinese peasants. Ping remembered sitting on her father's lap when she was about four years old tracing her hands over the rough fabric of his jacket, fingering the five large buttons down the front. The pockets were so deep she could put her arm in up to her elbow, then draw out a sweet or coin.

The jacket was a symbol of the freedom of the Chinese people. After the Manchus invaded and overthrew the Ming dynasty they oppressed the Chinese for hundreds of years. They inflicted the hateful queue, the long plait hanging down the back, that every Chinese man was forced to wear. Those who had refused had been executed. The hero Sun Yat Sen led a rebellion that culminated in 1912 when the emperor was overthrown and the republic established. He instigated the outfit of a simple peaked cap, jacket and plain trousers in dark blue material as the national dress and it soon became a symbol of support for Chairman Mao and his promise of something better for China's peasants.

The man in front of Ping on the bus had his cap fixed firmly on his head, accentuating his large ears. She could not see his face, but by the slope of his shoulders and the worn Mao jacket, guessed him to be the same age as her father. Like Mao's promises, the jacket was now threadbare and faded. Ping let her head drop forward, close to the man's back. There it was – the same smell of earth, sweat and tobacco that reminded her of her father. Her eyes moistened at the memory. Several years earlier, he had left home to find work in the cities. Had he been forced to travel like this?

Home for Ping was a three-roomed house in a village of about thirty dwellings. Most of the villagers were able to make a living from their fields but her family's land was not very fertile. Her mother continued to struggle alone to produce some crops, but her father, like millions of others all over China, felt he had no other choice but to go to work as a labourer in the city over five hundred kilometres away. There was always work to be had on the hundreds of building sites as the old cities expanded and new ones sprang up.

At first Ping's father had come home every two months, but his visits had become less and less frequent. These days he would only come home at Spring Festival – that is if his employer did not cheat him. She remembered his miserable homecoming two years ago; when with tears in his eyes he ranted against the construction company bosses who had absconded with his wages just before the holiday. But even then he had bought some small presents with the little money he had obtained – Ping didn't want to think how he had got it, but she thought she knew. Fathers could not lose face in the family and many felt driven to theft.

It had been months since she had seen him. Now she was being separated from her mother and brothers too. They had stood on the narrow station platform as she boarded the train, but she had not been able to get close enough to the window to wave. She pictured her twin brothers, Xiao Han and Xiao Feng, waving frantically, hoping she was able to see them.

The bus gradually emptied along the route and Ping was no longer protected by the crush of bodies. She grabbed a strap and held on tightly to prevent herself from being thrown about. The extra space did nothing to relieve the oppressive heat – even the breeze was dry and stifling.

From her new vantage point she surveyed the other passengers. On Ping's left, the lady's blotchy complexion
testified to her attempt to change her tanned peasant's
skin to a 'city' colour. White skin was believed to be a
mark of superior breeding and Chinese women of
wealth took great pains to keep their skin as pale as possible. Most carried a parasol and female cyclists would
wear a thin white cape around their shoulders and
attach it to the handlebars to prevent their arms, hands
and knees from being exposed to the sun's rays. To protect the face, most wore a plastic, brown-coloured peak
fastened round the back of their heads. Brown skin
spoke of inferior status, and no eligible male would wish
to associate with it. Should any traces of tanning appear,
whitening creams were used to change the offending
parts. Ping's mother had spoken scathingly of the practice, saying laughingly, 'Being white can cover three
shades of ugliness.'

Some girls at Ping's school had used whitening
creams to try and hide their peasant origins. Ping had
tried it once but had later felt guilty at trying to be better than her mother. There was something to be proud of
in being a peasant after all – it was the peasants who had
provided the vital force Chairman Mao had used to
overthrow the Nationalists. Without the peasants the
masses would still be oppressed.

As the passengers on the bus gradually spread out, Ping
was able to peer out the window. She could see the city
buildings, most of which were ugly grey blocks of concrete.
From her position she couldn't see how high they were, but
she had a sense they were huge. Many of the shop signs
had words written in a Roman script like 'boutique' and
'fashion shoes' and Ping wondered how many people
could understand them. Traffic swelled around the bus as

it rumbled along its route, a steady stream of cars, motor cycles, buses, lorries and even tractors vied with each other, none going very fast because of the congestion.

There was nothing new in seeing bikes weaving in and out of the trucks and tractors, but Ping had never seen so many of them: there were hundreds and hundreds of cyclists, sometimes four abreast, even some individuals travelling in the opposite direction to the stream of traffic. Most cyclists rode unencumbered but some carried children and young people on the backs of their bikes, while others had a variety of packages wobbling unsteadily. She observed one man who had strapped a refrigerator to the side of his bike and was leaning to the other side as he cycled to counterbalance its weight. One or two cyclists pulled little carts with seats inside. She noticed an elderly man bending low over the pedals to use all his weight to pull a cart containing an even more elderly woman, sitting sedately and quite unafraid despite the mêlée around her. As Ping's bus inched slowly across the cycle lane and into a bus stop, the river of cyclists squeezed towards the pavement, then slowed and split, some going round the side of the bus to take their chance with the traffic while others still tried to edge between the bus and the pavement. Several times she watched, aghast, as passengers stepped off the bus and collided with a cyclist trying to get through the narrow gap.

She braced herself for the inevitable lurching as the bus came to her stop. She let go of the strap, lifted her bag, and pushed her way through the crowd of passengers to get to the exit. The two doors swung open and she bumped the bag down the steep steps. She put it down, looking at the throngs of people. The entrance loomed above her, 'Shencheng Agricultural University' carved in the concrete.

From: Jon Perrywell
Sent: July 2004
Subject: Crouching Tiger, Hidden Jon

Hello everyone,

This is just a quick update. I'm shortly going to be heading off to China for a year to teach English at Shencheng Agricultural University. My own days at uni are now sadly over, but I'm really looking forward to everything.

I'm leaving on 21 July, going to Thailand for some 'living in Asia' orientation, then flying to China on 30 July. I should be back next July–August time. It's turning out to be amusing enough already: as most of you know, I'm barely fluent in English myself, and I'm going with a Scottish guy, so spare a thought for those poor Chinese students who are going to end up with some random mixed-up Black Country/Scottish accent!

Thus, there's great potential for fun and interesting times. I'd love to share these with you. So here's how:

1. You can still get hold of me on my normal email address. The deal is this: my mum is going to be looking after the account, forwarding emails on to me, censoring them if necessary. This is because the Chinese government can easily read emails coming to foreigners in China, and they tend to get suspicious if you mention sensitive issues such as human rights, Tibet, Christianity, etc. So, not wishing to sound too '007' about it, please be careful to whom you show any of my emails. And don't send anything to this account that you wouldn't want my mum to read.

You can also send me real post via my home address, but same restrictions apply: don't mention anything you wouldn't want my mum or the Chinese government to read . . .

2. I'm planning to send out an occasional email to keep in touch. These will probably contain general news of what I'm up to, how I'm getting on, any problems or funny situations I have got into, and so on. Also, if you would like to pray for me whilst I'm away (and please do – I'm not going to be able to make it alone), email me back. Don't get your hopes up regarding entertainment value though. The best you can expect is bad puns about the Ming Temple. I'm not funny. Deal with it.

Lastly, if any of you are around this week, I'm going to be having a kind of leaving-party type-thing at mine on Wednesday. Let me know if you want to come.

Anyway, that's enough about me. Sorry for the group email, but hopefully catch up before I leave.

Jon

2.

Shencheng Agricultural University was by no means the oldest nor most prestigious of the city's universities. Whereas one of them had just celebrated its ninetieth anniversary, SAU was barely twenty years old, having been set up in the eighties in the rush to develop China and open it up to the world after decades of isolation. As the bus pulled away, Ping stood exhausted, staring up at the university gates. She was relieved to have made it relatively unscathed and nothing could diminish her pleasure and pride that she had actually arrived.

She was the only one from her senior school to have chosen this university. Eleven out of her class of fifty had graduated with scores in excess of 532 – the minimum necessary for college entrance. She needed 548 for this college and had scored 550. She could get a respectable degree here and after that – well, who knew what the future held? She put down her large multi-coloured plastic bag of belongings and studied the impressive buildings. This was so much nicer than her village with its run-down houses of brown, baked clay and endless, dusty and uneven roads. But, she reminded herself, that was home.

A taxi screeched to a stop and Ping turned to watch a young man emerge. She had not seen such a smartly dressed man before, especially one so young. His hair was all spiky and he was wearing a light blue shirt over striped trousers. His shoes were white and red with buckles, and looked brand new. So different from the drab blacks and greys of the practical clothes her friends in the village wore.

Coming back for his second academic year – a sophomore, as they were now calling themselves – Beng Chu enjoyed the feeling of higher status. He also enjoyed the stares of the peasant girl, presumably a freshman, who had evidently just arrived full of excitement, and probably totally new to the city. He gave the taxi driver twenty yuan and slammed the door.

'Hello,' he beamed. 'Do you want some help? This'll be your first day I suppose, so you'll need to report at the office.'

Ping, a little flustered by his attention but secretly pleased, responded in the expected way, 'You're very kind but it's OK, I can manage.'

Beng had anticipated this customary refusal (to accept any kind of offer immediately was considered rude) and he didn't want to go through another round of offer and refusal.

'No, I insist,' he said breezily, 'and I only have a small bag myself.'

With that Beng heaved the girl's bag onto his shoulder and began walking away. After a respectable pause he turned to her again.

'Where are you from?' he enquired.

'My home is in a small village,' she replied.

'Is it far away?' Though Beng had lived all his life in the province, he had only ever passed through the rural villages on his way to a bigger city or tourist attraction.

'About three hours.' Distances tended to be measured by the time taken on the train. He pictured in his mind what she had endured sitting or more likely standing for three hours in a crowded compartment in this heat.

'And what department will you be in?' he asked.

'Well, I had hoped to get into the Trade Department but I have been put in with the English majors.'

'Really!' He laughed with genuine pleasure. 'That's where I am – I'm in my second year.'

Ping smiled at him. He was thin-faced and in spite of his cheerfulness, had serious eyes. His spiky hair seemed to match the way his ears stuck out. He was not handsome in her opinion but she took an instant liking to him. After that lonely and uncomfortable journey it was nice to meet someone so affable. But remembering her mother's caution about young men in the city, she decided to change the subject, 'I suppose you live near here?'

The taxi ride, the smart clothes and small bag indicated that he had not come far. He grinned, realizing she had quickly sized him up, 'I live with my parents in an apartment quite near the city centre.'

What he didn't want to tell her was that his father was a Party official and his mother had a small stationery shop. Beng was an only child – like most of his city friends – and lacked for nothing. By her standards he was incredibly rich, but he didn't want to overawe this sweet country girl. He had often wondered what life consisted of when your parents were just peasants. He had heard that country folk resented being tied by birth to the land, in poverty and ignorance, and he knew most of his city friends looked down on the peasant class. The two of them came from different worlds.

Beng looked at the bag he was carrying for Ping and tried to guess what was in it. Probably just cheap clothes and some extra blankets. By contrast, just now, in the taxi, he had been thinking it was a pity he could not bring his electric guitar to the small dormitory he shared with six others. Life at college presented few opportunities to perform and develop his talent. This was the only cloud on Beng's otherwise bright horizon. Music was his first love. When he had shown talent as a child, his parents had pushed him quite hard to develop it, and lessons and regular practice were added to a busy schedule of schoolwork. In their view the old adage, '*a book holds a house of gold*', extended to every form of knowledge, in science, arts or business. Some day there would be a payback for all that learning. But Beng's father was adamant that Beng should pursue a 'proper' career, so music was now relegated to a hobby.

However, his scores in academic subjects were not encouraging, which was why he had ended up at SAU and not a more prestigious university. Life could be worse though: he was the class monitor, which kept him a bit too busy, but earned him the respect of the class. It also put him on good terms with the university Party Secretary who was said to be on a steep career path. That would be useful one day as his father constantly reminded him.

Beng pointed out to Ping where the new students enrolled and resolved to keep his questions on neutral ground – about her schooling and hobbies. He was amused by the girl's pronounced country dialect, which crept into her standard Mandarin from time to time. Like almost half China's population, the people in Ping's village conversed daily in one of the other eighty Chinese dialects. Many could not even speak Mandarin, and so Ping would switch from the standardized Mandarin she had learnt at school to her traditional dialect quite unconsciously. This was much to Beng's confusion as he struggled to recognize the words she used.

'Are the teachers strict?' Ping asked.

'Not really. I think you'll find life a bit more relaxed here than at the middle school. We're also going to have a foreign teacher who will be taking us for some of the English classes this year. The foreigners are usually very nice, but have some strange ways,' Beng replied.

From: Jon Perrywell
Sent: August 2004
Subject: All Thai'd Up

Hello!

If you're reading this email it's because you've asked me to keep you up to date with what I'm getting up to over the next year. So here goes . . .

At the moment I'm in Chiang Mai, Thailand having just finished some orientation for my forthcoming year in China. This basically involved staying in a swish but cheap hotel (called the Porn Ping) and meeting lots of people, mostly Brits and Americans. I've met the two people who are going to the same city as me, Simon is from Scotland and I'll be sharing a flat with him, and Charlotte is a primary teacher from Cambridge. I think we're going to have a blast.

Anyway. Thailand. Chiang Mai is a beautiful place but it's full of westerners and I think the city has become a bit of a gap year cliché. So what better place to start out from? Aside from orientation, I've been eating lots of random food (mango sticky rice is the best), visiting an elephant farm, learning a bit of Mandarin (very confusing), and watching bad Thai TV (though we do get BBC World in the hotel rooms – I'm going to miss that in China, where the government has blocked even the BBC website out. I always suspected that *The Archers* was counter-revolutionary propaganda). We had the chance to chat to some Theravada monks. (Theravada is the oldest surviving school of Buddhism.

About 70 per cent of the Thai population adheres to its teachings. Or so I'm told.) Today we went to the zoo, which was quite a random and tiring experience. Think a British zoo but with the cages about three miles apart . . .

OK, so that's it for the minute. Tomorrow we're off to China, staying overnight in Kunming. Then on Friday we're flying to Shencheng, which will be my home for the next year. Shencheng, a city of seven million in central China is apparently the Cleveland, Ohio, of China. Make of that what you will. From tomorrow onwards hotmail is out of bounds to me and my mum's going to be forwarding anything you send to this account, so bear that in mind.

I hope the British summer is treating you well ☺

God bless,

        Jon

3.

The temperature was around thirty degrees Celsius with no breeze to mitigate the oppressive heat. Ping reckoned she had been practising marching exercises for at least three hours. The baggy army fatigues she was compelled to wear now clung to her sticky body and made her feel stupid. She was hot and thirsty, her back ached, and she was beginning to get angry.

She had known that the first weeks at university would involve military training but she hated being shouted at and made to march and practise drills. She had approached the four weeks of training philosophically, believing it to be a necessary prelude to academic life. However after two weeks of it, the exhaustion, frustration and boredom eroded her resolve and she slipped into despondency. She groaned inwardly, wondering how long it would be before she could get her heavy boots off, have a cold drink and relax on her bed in the dormitory.

The regimen was based on army training and army instructors were drafted in to implement the daily routines. All the freshmen were summoned at 5 a.m. each morning and had to make their beds in the prescribed form. The instructors constantly reminded them they were kids no more and were now entering the adult world where they could not expect to be coddled by their mothers. They would need to look after themselves, keep the dormitories and classrooms spotless, and do their own laundry. There were inspections of their uniforms, beds and rooms every day and anyone failing to come up to the prescribed standard got punishment exercises – normally running round the sports track until they were close to exhaustion.

The others in Ping's dormitory had been eager to get into their uniforms and were obviously in no hurry to begin classes. They thought it was great fun to dress up, join the freshman boys, and parade around the campus to the stares and shouts of encouragement of the older students. Ping did not share their enthusiasm.

'Sing up,' shouted their class monitor.

They were marching in ranks, four abreast, seven ranks to a class, with the monitor at the back. She appeared to have been chosen for the volume of noise she could produce and it had the desired effect of boosting their flagging morale – except for Ping. This was like being back at school: shouting slogans about Mother China and the Party. She was not disloyal – far from it – she was as proud of her country as the other students and admired and respected their leaders. At school she had enjoyed the thrilling stories of the revolutionary pioneers like Sun Yat Sen, Chairman Mao, and Deng Xiaoping. And she enjoyed the comradeship and sense of excitement of being part of the huge project of making China great again. But she objected to this constant drilling and marching. Each day consisted of various forms of physical training and endurance. Two days ago they had to sit on the grass on the sports field for an hour in the hot sun.

Some of the other girls enjoyed the physical challenge and desperately wanted to prove themselves as strong as the boys. Ping suspected these were probably city girls who enjoyed the novelty of it. But she had had her fill of physical challenges – the daily drudgery of working in the fields with her mother – and now hoped university would set her on a different course. She mentally braced herself and reminded herself she would get through it. She pictured her mother's sweating, lined face and remembered the many times she had said *'To survive you have to learn to eat bitterness.'*

Mei Li heard the singing from the third floor of her dormitory and leaned out of the window to watch the parading students as they came round the corner. She loved the songs and their exuberance. The ranks and ranks of these young people were like the never-ending river of life, a conduit of new blood into their massive nation. At least that's what the president of the university had said. She began waving and shouting to encourage them. Many looked up and grinned, then snapped their heads forward, and strode on with new vigour. Feeling the excitement she joined in the song 'I love China' and her enthusiasm was so infectious the others in the dormitory joined her at the window, singing and shouting until the marchers disappeared from view.

'Hold on guys, here's another bunch of them,' Beng shouted, as he ran up behind his two friends. Both were shorter than him and dressed less fashionably though they too had wealthy parents. One was conspicuous by the ginger tinge to his dyed hair, while the other was plump and wore a perpetual smile which accentuated the dimples in his cheeks. The three boys could hear the singing marchers long before the freshmen appeared round the corner of the library building with their eyes fixed forward to the drill leader and their arms swinging to full shoulder height. They were obviously enjoying themselves and sang happily. The boys stepped back off the road and waited at the side, watching.

'Look, someone still doesn't know his right from his left.'

The three sophomores looked to where their friend was pointing and tried to hold back their laughter at a tall, stiff-limbed guy who seemed totally uncoordinated and hopped from one foot to the other to correct his stride. It was then they noticed the girl behind him, marching with her head held high, her long silky hair flowing from under the army cap. She was tall and incredibly attractive, with a sensuous face and full lips. Her skin was well tanned like the other marchers, after days spent outside. From the set of her unsmiling jaw and her narrowed eyes, she was obviously not enjoying the experience. Her mouth barely opened to sing the words of the song.

'Will you just look at that – where on earth did that beauty come from?' the ginger-haired boy whispered, nudging his friend. 'Isn't that your peasant friend, Beng?'

Ping stiffened as she recognized Beng's face beaming at her from the pavement. She pretended not to notice him and stared straight ahead as the colour rose to her cheeks. They had only met a couple of times since his taxi had drawn up behind her but she enjoyed his company. She knew he would be talking about her to his friends. How embarrassing to be seen like this!

Beng blinked in astonishment. He had only seen Ping in the cheap clothes she had brought from the country and their inferior quality was obvious when he saw her alongside richer students. But now that all the students were dressed the same the ill-fitting army fatigues seemed to accentuate the girl's beauty. Beng grinned in delight. But as he saw her blush, he realized how embarrassed she was and quickly ushered his friends away.

Out of the corner of her eye Ping saw Beng and his friends leave. Thank heaven, she thought. It was bad enough being seen in clothes that seemed so shabby compared to those of his other friends and she must have looked even more stupid in this ill-fitting garb. Ping realized how much she wanted to impress him.

As the three boys made their way to a table in the crowded canteen, Beng could not get the image of Ping out of his mind. It was not her looks, though her beauty had startled him – it was her expression, almost like anguish. Why did the freshmen have to waste four weeks like this when they could have begun classes? Supposedly the object of the training was not that they should be soldiers but the requirement to wear combat fatigues seemed to him to send a subtle message. Students should be ready to defend the Middle Kingdom if called upon to do so. What they were doing was not just physical training. No one could miss the echoes of the revolutionary struggle. Was this the right message? That the solution to China's problems was to be found in physical power? The strict discipline just tried to press everyone into the same mould.

Beng could feel his resentment rising: how are you supposed to cope with being squeezed into a mould you could never fit? The world was such a big place and opportunities outside China were endless. Why should he simply accept the dictates of his father? But the alternative

– to cause his father to lose face by confronting him –
seemed impossible.

✦

As he ambled past the university buildings towards the
main gate, Wang Dan did not hear the marchers until
they were a few metres away and several onlookers had
to shout to get his attention. He looked up and quickly
leapt out of the way.

As Wang stood there peering at the ranks upon ranks
of students in their army uniforms he had a flashback to
his days at school, all the children wearing their red
Young Pioneers scarves, singing songs and chanting
'Always be prepared' in answer to the teacher's lead: *'Be
prepared to struggle for the cause of communism.'*

Joining the Young Pioneers was one of the first rites of
passage of the school experience. Coming home from his
first day Wang had been proud of his little red scarf,
showing it off to his parents and continually checking it
was properly tied. No doubt all the children felt this
same sense of honour and distinction even though millions passed through the ranks of the official youth
movement each year.

Wang calculated it was six years since he had last
marched with the Pioneers. Some of his classmates had
enrolled in the Communist Youth League but he had
declined. He still remembered the YP promise: *'Under
the Pioneers Flag I promise that: I love the Communist Party
of China, I love the Motherland, and I love the people: I will
study well and keep fit to prepare to contribute my effort to the
cause of communism.'* He had certainly tried to keep fit,
but – study well? On the other hand here he was in the
fourth year of a university degree so he had obviously
met the requirements of the system.

At 1.82 metres he was among the tallest in his year. His muscular body came from a summer of tough labour on his parents' farm in the west of the province. His family's farmland had proved quite fertile and being close to the city, his father grew vegetables for the city market and had become reasonably prosperous. University was his ticket to something better though and he hoped one day to provide his parents with more than just physical labour. He had a square jaw and deep set eyes and something about his face always made him appear to be on the verge of laughter. He had resisted the modern trend of keeping his hair short mainly because he was proud of his unusually wavy hair.

This was Wang's final year in International Marketing, and in the second term he would have to start seriously considering his job options. He had returned to college three days ago in part to have a rest from farm work before classes began, but mainly to look out for Lin Yang, a third year student in his department with whom he had developed a close friendship last year. He had tried to speak to her a few times during the holiday using a phone in the village but every time he called, her father would turn him away, saying Lin was not available. Her father obviously disapproved of Wang – a mere farmer's son.

Wang recalled the last time he had phoned; desperately hoping Lin herself would answer.

'Wei, hello.'

Wang's heart sank when he heard the stiff bass voice of her father. 'Hello Mr Yang, may I speak to Lin please?'

'Who are you?' was the curt response.

'My name is Wang. I am at the same college as Lin.'

'I'm afraid she is not available to speak to you.'

'But I have rung three times and she never seems to be available – is she ill?'

There was a brief silence. Wang realized he had made a serious blunder in asking if Lin was ill: parents might take offence at the mere suggestion that they were unable to look after their children. He waited anxiously for a response, desperately hoping the silence meant that Lin was being summoned to the phone.

Mr Yang spoke again, slowly and pointedly. 'Wang, let me explain two things. First, my daughter has always been well looked after in my home and is in excellent health. Secondly and you'll pardon my bluntness, I don't care how many times you have rung because I will decide when she is available and to whom. You would be wise not to waste your time and money in future. Goodbye.'

Wang was thinking of Lin as he jumped out the way of the marchers and walked along behind them, before turning to head for the main entrance. He went to one of the public phones near the main gate and dialled Lin's dormitory. The dormitories they shared gave students little privacy.

The phone rang four times before one of the girls answered it. She recognized Wang's voice. 'No luck, I'm afraid. Lin's not back from class yet,' the girl informed him.

'Please tell her to phone me when she's in.'

He replaced the receiver and walked away as another student came to use it. He wandered gloomily back through the entrance. He had met Lin twice since she returned to the campus and both times he felt a greater distance between them. She was polite and friendly and they shared stories about things that had happened in the holidays, but it left him feeling empty. At their last meeting when he finally asked her if her feelings for him had changed she looked down at her clasped hands.

After a long silence she almost whispered, 'I don't know.'

'Is it your father?' he asked, half expecting her agreement.

'I . . . I can't talk about it,' she blurted out. 'I must go and prepare for tomorrow.' And with that she got up and hurried away.

From: Jon Perrywell
Sent: September 2004
Subject: The Laowai Has Landed

Hello folks,

It's a warm and wet Tuesday afternoon in Shencheng and I've been in China for nearly four weeks. My toothpaste is beginning to run out – that's as good a reason as any to say hello and give you a little update from the Middle Kingdom.

So I'm living in Shencheng which is a whopping great city in the middle of China. Shencheng is the capital city of the province. It is absolutely mind-blowing. With seven million people, it's nearly as big as London. It's very busy – most people get around by foot, bike or bus and the traffic is absolutely crazy, as is the pollution.

Shencheng is usually covered in a layer of fine white dust from the Gobi desert and the many building sites, as well as pollution from all the cars and scooters. It means I've got itchy eyes and an itchy nose nearly permanently, and that keeping my flat dust-free is like painting the Forth Bridge!

A large chunk of Shencheng resembles a building site with forests of cranes. They are building a new development which aims to double the size of the city. As if seven million people weren't enough. There are loads of futuristic skyscrapers and they're banging up more of them all the time. In China, tall buildings aren't ghettoized in the city centre, they're everywhere. They don't do suburbs here: the tower blocks start where the countryside ends, and everyone lives in flats. It is all rather strange. Having been to Nairobi last year, I expected Shencheng to be similarly surrounded by sprawling slums, or at least some kind of suburb. Instead there is an almost perfect boundary between the city and the country. Apparently China has what is known as the *Hukou* system. Every Chinese citizen is registered as either a rural or an urban resident. Rural residents have no right of residence, housing, education or healthcare in urban areas. On the one hand this has helped prevent the build-up of massive slums on the edges of Chinese cities (as has happened in Africa, Latin America, or south Asia). On the other, it has condemned rural dwellers to second-class citizenship in a system which one report described as 'peasant apartheid'.[1] Nowadays, millions of rural dwellers do migrate to the cities, but this migration is usually temporary, resulting in a 'floating population' of migrant workers numbering an estimated one hundred and forty-four million[2] They form one of the most impoverished groups in society.

Also, there are very few foreigners here; when I'm out in the city I can't read anything or speak to anyone and it can sometimes feel a bit alienating. My first cycle ride into the city centre (only about thirty minutes away) was overwhelming: massive buildings emblazoned with bright adverts in incomprehensible Chinese characters; the searing dusty August heat; constant noise from traffic, sirens, construction works and loudspeakers; and lots and lots and lots and lots and lots of people, with whom I had no way of communicating. When I got back to my flat the information overload was just too much and I had to go and lie down. I felt like my brain was going to dribble out of my ears. I feel a bit like I am living in a state of constant confusion as to what is going on; in terms of language, I am basically deaf, mute and illiterate. When people approach me I have no way of telling whether their intentions are good or ill, so it is hard not to be suspicious and cold towards strangers. The result of all this is that basic daily activities leave me feeling knackered.

I'm trying to learn Chinese and now know a few basics but I usually have to resort to wild gestures and my handy phrasebook. We have a good laugh. Sometimes.

This year I'm going to be teaching English on the Shencheng Agricultural University (SAU) campus. I had been expecting to be only teaching university students but now I'm also taking some middle school classes. These started last Saturday and I've really enjoyed my first week. The teenagers are a good laugh – stereotypical moody British teenagers they are not.

The university classes don't start until early October because the students have got four weeks of military training first. Several thousand of them arrived a couple of weeks ago and since then I've been watching them parading around the campus in strictly regimented blocks, wearing identical tracksuits and camouflage T-shirts, and chanting patriotically. It's all very communist and a bit intimidating. After growing used to (albeit still not understanding) adverts for McDonald's and Pepsi and other visible manifestations of the high rate of economic development and international openness, watching the military training has brought it home with a loud 'thunk' that China is still ruled by the Communist Party. Britain is obsessed with its recent history in which the threat of a totalitarian regime was very real and I find these military displays quite frightening. Still, I can't help being amused in an *'Allo 'Allo* kind of way, and bemused by the sheer anachronism of a globalized society run by a communist party.

Simon, my fellow English teacher, and I are living in a great flat on the SAU campus in the foreign teachers' building. It's wonderful, and we're really not lacking anything materially (except Blu-Tack; for some reason they don't have it in China). We had it cleaned this morning, so the dust is no longer ankle deep. We're well supported by lots of Christian friends who live or work nearby. They've been terrific, taking us shopping and out for dinner, and inviting us round for DVDs.

China is very cheap. The exchange rate is about 15 yuan (which everybody calls 'kuai', pronounced 'kw – eye') to the pound. My bike was 180 kuai, a bowl of noodles would set you back 5 kuai and a nice meal about 15 kuai.

Anyway, I promised not to go on too long, so I'll end things there. Please let me know how things are back in England.

A few things to be praying about:

- In the midst of the excitement of moving to China and teaching my first lessons, I will keep focused on what's really important, and keep the Main Thing the main thing.
- Tiredness. I've been feeling really lethargic. Apparently this is normal, caused by the stress of moving to a new place and culture, etc. Pray that I'll regain energy soon.
- Safety. Shencheng's meant to be pretty safe in terms of crime. Unfortunately, the same can't be said of its traffic which is erratic to say the least. Please pray that I will be protected from harm and my own bad cycling.
- I will be able to develop genuine friendships with Chinese people (students mostly) and be able to start sharing the good news with them.

Love

Jon

4.

It was a beautiful evening. The moon was up and in its first quarter. Having lived here in the city for a month Ping appreciated the rare opportunity to be able to look up into such an unpolluted sky. Even a few stars were visible. This was like the sky she was used to seeing from the bedroom window back home. Grey skies and polluted haze hung over Shencheng most of the time. On some days, the smog was so bad she was unable to see the thirty-storey apartment blocks about five kilometres away. There was national concern about pollution but in the race for modernization, pollution from factories seemed a small price to pay. Shencheng was layered with dust, the air in all of China's cities was thick with fumes and China's rivers and lakes were filthy. The problem was hard to ignore. One did not need to look far to witness water pollution first hand – Ping had noticed the stream running along the northern boundary of the campus where the new dormitories had been built. It reeked and at times the disgusting smells wafted through the dormitories. The parlous state of the environment was likely to have serious consequences in the future. However Ping was sure the national leaders would find ways to solve these problems.

The dormitory Ping was assigned to had been a pleasant surprise, though she was disappointed that it wasn't actually on the campus. Ten months ago the university administration had been instructed to expand and take in another five thousand students as part of the drive to supply more and more graduates with the skills to support China's burgeoning industry. A site across the road from the main entrance had been identified and the owners of the land were 'invited' to build more dormitory blocks. Rumour had it that the land belonged to farmers who had good guanxi (influence from a relationship or a favour given) with someone in government. But fortunes change and this someone had clearly lost his influence. The farmers marched to the provincial offices, produced a banner and stood outside the entrance, airing their grievances to any who would listen (as happened all over China as the authorities pushed ahead with economic development and took over farmland). The situation had been resolved though with a little extra compensation.

The new dormitories were considerably larger than those on the main campus built to old standards. The new ones were wider, allowing a table to be positioned between the bunk beds so every student had space to study. All the toilets had functioning doors (unlike on the campus where doors that fell off were not repaired but simply discarded) and there were more sinks to wash clothes. Ping shared her dormitory with three girls, all of whom were in the English department. She was the oldest of the four: unlike the others she had missed a year of schooling when her mother had been taken ill.

Ping and her friend Zhao stopped on their way back from the bathhouse on the main campus, and gazed up into the sky. It was a wonderful feeling, to stand there relaxed in the cool clean air, the four gruelling weeks of army training now behind them and the week's holiday coming up.

'I hope we have clear skies this month,' Zhao whispered, trying not to break the special moment.

'Yes – that would be a real *Zhongqiujie*,' agreed Ping. *Zhongqiujie*, known as the Moon Festival, was shortly to take place.

'Are you going back home for the holiday?' Zhao asked.

'No, it costs too much – I was too late to get the cheap rail tickets. They only started selling tickets yesterday and when I arrived there was a huge queue already. I waited for a long time but they were sold out when I got to the window. How about you?'

'My dad will come and drive me home after Saturday's classes,' Zhao replied, almost apologetically.

The students did not always have classes on Saturdays, but 1 October, the PRC National Day and the traditional mid-autumn festival were next week. State companies and institutions gave their workers three paid 'official' holidays for the festival, and the government rearranged the surrounding weekends so that workers could enjoy seven days of holiday. It wasn't so much about kindness to employees though as about the billions of yuan in revenue that resulted. Similar arrangements were made for the Spring Holiday at the Chinese New Year, and the May Holiday.

The extended holiday made it possible to travel long distances to visit friends and family and the trains were usually jammed full. Rail tickets were only sold about three days before the journey so huge queues formed at ticket booths as Ping had discovered. Even if Ping had secured a ticket home, returning to Shencheng would have been a problem. For the majority of journeys only a one-way ticket could be purchased. So, to make a short visit someone at the other end would have to attempt to book your return journey. Obviously those prepared to pay a premium could book through travel agents who block-booked seats but Ping simply couldn't afford it. She had been surprised to discover how some of her classmates travelled – having actually booked a particular seat on a train or paid for a berth in the sleeper compartments. Some had even travelled in aeroplanes.

On the Friday evening before the week's holiday, there was a special gathering at the university. This was the formal celebration hosted by the Party Secretary to mark National Day. The university president, various deans and assistant deans, the Party Secretaries in each of the faculties, their assistants and the class monitors were all invited as were the retired teachers and Party cadres who lived on the campus.

Beng was seated among the class monitors and looked round at the dignitaries. This was only the second time he had been invited to the anniversary celebrations and he found himself awed by the event. Beng heard a boy behind him grumbling under his breath – obviously not all the class monitors shared Beng's enthusiasm about being there. Beng ignored him and his well-worn comments – there were dissidents everywhere.

After a choir had sung some well-loved Party songs, the president began his speech, thanking everyone, especially the Party, without which they would still be oppressed by the emperors or caught up in civil war. That was the cue for the Party Secretary to stand and recite a speech he had given many times before: the wonderful contribution made by the Party to the betterment of the nation; the many recent initiatives in education to ensure that more young people enjoyed tertiary education; the exciting but challenging opportunities that existed for the best performers and loyal Party workers; the possibility that some here might even be sponsored for overseas education. Beng listened intently. It is the responsibility of all Party members to safeguard the Constitution; uphold the socialist road, the people's democratic dictatorship, and leadership by the Communist Party of China; protect Marxist-Leninism-Mao Zedong Thought, and Deng Xiaoping Theory; and persevere in the Reform and Opening policy. Even to Beng this was well-worn rhetoric of which the Party Secretary reminded them every term.

From: Jon Perrywell
Sent: October 2004
Subject: Teacher Jon

A big *nimen hao* ☺[3]

Time for instalment number two. I can't quite recall when I sent you the last one but so much stuff has happened in between now and then that I'm going to send another.

So, my interesting times in the Middle Kingdom . . .

We got to be in the audience of a TV chat show a couple of weeks ago. A colleague was dragged into it as a token white person. Chinese chat shows aren't as wild and debauched as their Japanese counterparts: this one was on the topic of foreign residence permits. And yes, it was every bit as interesting as it sounds. All three hours of it.

Turning on the television in China yields a bewildering array of channels. My lifeline is Deutsche Welle, the German equivalent of the BBC, whose comfortingly Eurocentric reports are a breath of fresh air, even if the stories covered aren't always the most scintillating. ('The SDP have been voted out in Schleswig-Holstein.' Great.) The other English-language channel is CCTV 9, whose sycophantic drivel is too bad for words. CCTV, the centrally controlled broadcaster (appropriately named, no?) has several other channels, as does the provincial TV station. There are numerous specialist ones for sport, music, culture, health, the military and legal affairs. It was the last channel which was broadcasting our wonderful chat show.

The incident illustrates how easy it is for white foreigners to become micro-celebrities in Shencheng. There are so few of us here that we attract lots of curiosity, amusement and frequent ridicule. You can't go out on the street without someone staring and shouting 'Hello!' or '*Laowai!*' (literally 'Old Outsider', a colloquial but not derogatory term for foreigner) at you.

Last Friday was a public holiday for National Day, which celebrates the communist liberation (*sic*) of China in 1949, and begins a week's public holiday, rather like our October half-term. Basically the whole country is on holiday for a week and at the last count over one hundred million Chinese decided to get away. So imagine an extreme version of the British bank holiday travel nightmare and you won't be far off. Apparently it made a tidy sum of 46 billion yuan (5.8 billion US dollars) in revenue the last time they checked, so I can see why the government call it a 'Golden Week'. We had a picnic in the local park, followed by a bit of busking to promote the English Corner we run on Saturday evenings. The English Corner is basically a chance for anyone to turn up and practice their English on real *waiguoren* ('foreigners' but literally translates as 'outside country people'). It's a great chance for us to meet and chat with local people. But before we'd even touched the guitars our picnic was surrounded by about fifty gawkers who just stood there and unashamedly stared at the pale-skinned specimens, even asking for photos with us.

Celebrity status has its advantages and its drawbacks. On the plus side, you get a lot of attention from Chinese who are very friendly and often want to ask you all sorts of questions about Britain, life, etc. You get invited to stuff and get presents from the university. On the other hand, you often feel used as your hosts wheel you out like a performing animal or a freak show exhibit. And traders know they can rip you off good and proper.

Anyway, back to the park. We managed to hand out a lot of leaflets that day.

I spent the rest of the Golden Week off in Xi'an, the ancient capital of China, with a couple of friends. We saw the Terracotta Army and generally chilled. It was nice to have a break, but getting to and from Xi'an was an adventure in itself. On the way there we got an overnight 'hard sleeper' train. Think of a moving human battery farm and you wouldn't be far off. The bunk beds were three high and the pillows were solid foam bricks: you could have fractured someone's skull in a pillow fight. I was woken up by an old Chinese woman slapping the soles of my feet and jabbering very loudly at me (I was wearing earplugs and a sleep mask). I thought she was being rude but the train had got into Xi'an early and it turned out she was trying to be helpful. It still scared the noodles out of me. On the way back we weren't so fortunate; we had hard seat tickets. Hard seat is the class everyone advises you not to travel. The guidebook contains dire warnings about sharing a carriage with smoking, spitting peasants and their animals, and knife gangs who work the carriages at night. This impression is perpetuated by a recent film called *A World Without Thieves* (*Tianxia Wu Zei*), which fortunately I hadn't watched. Nothing of the sort transpired but I got very little sleep. It definitely put British Rail into perspective.

It is back to work now though. Last week my classes with the first-year students started after they'd finally finished goose-stepping around the yard. I discovered my bubble-wrapped, middle-class, English existence where conflict only happens at a distance had left me hypersensitive and the regimented rows of camouflage-clad youngsters had an air of Nuremberg rally about it. I had to remind myself that it was only sixty years ago that conscription was the norm in the UK. Anyway. I taught these freshers for the first time last week. They're an enthusiastic bunch, and seem to be quite a different crowd from the 'little emperors' (the over-indulged precious offspring of wealthy parents) I'm teaching at the middle school. Part of the first homework was to describe their hopes and fears for the future, and this gave me an insight into what makes them tick. They've come from all around the province, and seem relatively poor. They have high expectations and the pressure on them to succeed must be immense. They live in dormitories, eight to a room, with communal facilities and no hot water. I hope I can do my best to help them, but more importantly, to show them the One who can meet their every need.

I was told last week that the middle school no longer wants me to teach there. They have not been particularly forthcoming with their reasons for this, but we suspect it was more financial than a reflection on me. I hope. On the plus side, I now have more time in which to plan lessons, learn Chinese and get to know my students. Hopefully the English Corner we're running will help with that.

We are seeing God do some amazing stuff here. A couple of friends are studying the Bible with some students and two of them have recently given their lives to Jesus. We'd been praying about these people for quite a while, so it was a real answer to see them come to this point. I'm hopefully going to start another study with some of my students, beginning next week. Please be praying about this.

Also, a couple of Canadians have moved into our block. They're not Christians (to my knowledge) but we are praying that while they are here God will work on their hearts, and use us in this.

Ah, the most important British topic – the weather! It's suddenly got a bit colder but is still pleasant; I can turn my air con off and go out without sweating like a beast.

Well, I think I've given you enough to chew on for the time being.

> God bless,
> Jon

---

[3] Hello (plural).

5.

Education is a serious matter. Distractions are to be avoided and extra-curricular activities should not to be encouraged. Unless of course they can be justified.

The SAU English Corner gave students the opportunity to practise their English, so was easily justified, but the light-hearted atmosphere was so different from anything the university ran that the students actually enjoyed coming too. It was always well attended, and the westerners would be bombarded with often well-rehearsed and repeated questions: What did they think about China? Did they like Chinese food? How did they manage to buy things from the shops when they knew so little Mandarin? Why is London such a foggy place (as portrayed in the Dickens novels they studied)? But sometimes good discussion began despite the students' stunted English . . .

'Is money necessary for happiness?'

'Of course it is – how could we have got to university without it? And now that we're here we want to graduate and get well-paid jobs,' asserted one of the boys confidently.

'Yes,' agreed a girl, 'I want my parents to be happy. That's why I'll get a good job – so that one day I can look after them.' The girl who had just spoken was not from the countryside like Ping, where tradition still held it was the son's responsibility to care for his parents. Ping knew her parents had been relieved when her brothers were born and they had the promise of financial security, but had they been unhappy when it was just her? Wasn't it tradition rather than poverty that had led to her parents' unease?

'So all the peasants are unhappy, are they?' she blurted.

As the other students stared at her, Ping suddenly felt self-conscious. Life had been hard in her village, but she had been happy. Did you need to be rich to be happy? She wasn't sure.

'A good question,' said the first speaker, 'but if they were really content with what they've got would they bother to send their children to schools and universities to better themselves when it costs them so much? Most students I know from peasant families say that their parents don't want their children to have to stay on the land.'

Another student chipped in. 'But do they pay for their children to go to school and university to get a better life for the children themselves or so that their children will look after them better in their old age?' Coming from a wealthy family, he spoke from a disinterested, theoretical viewpoint.

Ping became angry. 'Of course not. My parents love me and want the best for me. I'll do the best for them but I'm not just their insurance policy.' She did not like anybody to speak about parents especially her own in this way. It was very disrespectful. Her outburst dealt a death blow to the discussion and an awkward silence filled the room.

'You must miss your family,' Mei said to the foreign teacher, steering the conversation back to a much safer subject.

'Yes, of course, but with email and telephones they don't seem so far away,' Jon replied, noticing Ping slipping out of the room.

'Do you think that western students are different from Chinese students?' asked Mei.

This was a common question and another foreign worker gave a non-committal reply: 'I suppose students all over the world are shaped by the culture they grow up in. So, for example, Chinese culture could be described as being more formal than western culture and that is reflected in the classroom. In class a Chinese student is expected to stand up to answer the teacher's question. That does not happen in the west.'

'Yes, I see,' said Mei, remembering Jon's first few classes where he had asked lots of questions. As the desk and seats were fixed together, the hinged seats needed to be raised in order to stand up. This would have been fine, but since the floor was considered a dirty place and bags could not be placed there, the students stuffed their bags behind them in their seats and these needed to be rearranged every time they got up. Mei giggled, remembering the commotion it had caused as the students bobbed up and down to answer the foreigner's questions.

'Do all the girls have boyfriends?' was Mei's next question.

'Not all of them.'

'I think it is very important to find a good husband. If he is ambitious a girl could be well looked after and become rich.'

The reply was predictable. The aim of many of the girls was to find a husband who had prospects: wealth and education were highly prized attributes. But in this quest to find a successful partner many young girls were duped by older men, already married and just looking for an affair. A rumour was currently flying around campus about Mr Luo, the university sports coach. He had been a fitness instructor in the Peoples Liberation Army before his appointment at the university. His parents had continued to nag him about taking a wife and eventually he had married a 'nice' girl from a good family in the city. However, the university was on the north side and rather than commuting daily, it was the norm to simply live near your work during the week and only return to your family home at the weekend. So, Mr Luo now lived in a room on the campus. He had been diligent in seeing his wife most weekends, but rumour had it that a student had caught his attention.

It had always seemed eminently sensible to Mei for the Party and government to recommend to its younger citizens that they should not follow the accepted norms of previous generations but should delay getting married. It would be much better to get educated and secure a good job then, with a reasonable amount of capital behind them, a couple could marry. They would be able to afford the good things in life including a decent education for their precious only child and put money aside for their pension as well as take care of aging parents. In this way society would benefit – ways needed to be found to reduce China's burgeoning population and to help the masses become less dependent on the state. And the boys Mei had met had not amounted to much. For the most part they seemed immature; few had a mind of their own and meekly allowed themselves to be guided by those in authority.

'Do you believe in God?' a foreigner asked.

Mei remembered the foreigners had said they were Christian, and replied rather dismissively, 'I don't know. I don't think so. It has never mattered to me whether God exists or not.'

'Well, I do. And I think it matters a great deal.'

Mei had stayed for two hours listening to the foreigners, several times challenging their statements quite fiercely. Back in the dormitory that evening when the chatter had died, Mei thought back over the issues they had covered. Staring up at the ceiling, the soft glow from a street light seeping through the curtains across the cracking paint, she whispered 'God, if you are there, I am prepared to believe in you, but I don't know how.'

6.

'How do you know all this?' asked Ping, staring at the computer screen.

Back home in her village it was only the government office that had a computer, so returning after Golden Week, Ping's friend Zhao had promised to take her to the computer room that evening and introduce her to the virtual world of the 'chat room'. Zhao was from another large city in the province, and apparently had her own computer at home. She did not look up but carried on typing as she answered Ping's question.

Sitting together in the narrow cubicle, Ping was fascinated as she watched her friend surf various sites and type and receive messages from people apparently many miles away. At least that's what she said she was doing. Zhao also said that she never gave anyone information about herself that was remotely true, so presumably others did the same and consequently no one knew who anybody really was, or where they lived! But Ping agreed with her – it was fun.

They linked up with specific people with whom Zhao often communicated and quite randomly found some new people to chat with. Judging by the number of students in the room it certainly seemed to be a popular pastime to Ping. She could well believe the stories that some students in her class were staying up late, sometimes into the early hours, glued to the screen.

'What do students write to each other about?' Ping asked.

'Everything and anything; lots about boyfriends or girlfriends. The latest songs – stuff like that.'

'Do you ever talk about important things?'

Her friend turned, looked at her and frowned. 'Boyfriends aren't important?' She then dropped her voice as she whispered, 'How about that cute boy next door?'

Ping shook her head and laughed. Zhao supplied the fun that Ping rarely allowed herself to enjoy. 'I don't mean that – you know what I mean. The serious things of life.'

Putting on a mock scared expression her friend said, 'Such as – what? Death?'

'No, of course not.'

There were certain subjects that one didn't speak about. Death was one of them. Ping pondered for a while, 'Well, such as – what's being done to help poor people in the west of China, or – maybe – when will Taiwan become reunited with the Mainland?'

'Not me!' Zhao replied firmly, 'but some do – let's ask.'

She looked around the room for a familiar face and shouted across to Wang, who told them an internet forum's address. She keyed it in and waited.

He put his head round the partition, 'Is it coming up?'

'It seems a bit slow,' replied Zhao, smiling broadly at him.

'Maybe it's been closed,' he suggested.

'Why would it be closed?' asked Ping.

'It was probably encouraging unsavoury subjects,' he said. 'Why not try the university bulletin board?'

Wang gave them the address and Ping asked if she could key it in this time.

Up it came on the screen. As they read through the various statements and opinions a new one appeared saying a shop that was rumoured to be selling bad meat was probably owned by provincial government officials.

'That's awful. I wonder if it's true,' said Ping indignantly.

Then a strange thing happened: the allegation about the officials suddenly disappeared.

'Something funny has happened on this bulletin board,' Zhao called to Wang. 'Someone wrote something and a minute later it disappeared.'

'That can happen – especially if it looks as if someone is trying to stir up trouble,' he explained, peering at their screen.

Ping frowned in puzzlement. 'But . . . how? Can anyone remove something that another person has written?'

'No – not just anyone – only the monitors.'

'You mean class monitors?' asked Ping.

Wang laughed at her innocence. 'No, no. The internet monitors.'

'Who?' Zhao asked incredulously.

'Just students who have been selected to work in the monitoring section.'

'But – do you know any?' Ping asked.

'Not for sure – but I have an idea who some might be. They're a bit like class monitors – keeping an eye on us to make sure nobody spreads wrong ideas. There are a lot of hotheads around you know. Anyway I must go.'

'I wonder if it's true,' said Zhao thoughtfully.

'What?'

'About the government official.'

Ping looked doubtful. 'It could be – but then again, it could be that someone has a grudge. Someone starts a rumour and before you know it the whole village believes it – people are like that.'

'Yes, but everyone is entitled to their opinions – isn't that the whole point about bulletin boards?' retorted Zhao.

'No one has a right to be wrong and mislead people.'

'I suppose so – but that works both ways, and who is to say what is right and what is wrong?'

Ping stared at her, puzzled that her friend would need to ask the question. 'Surely the Party knows that!'

Zhao burst out laughing then stopped suddenly as she realized she might have offended her friend. She smiled and said in a gentle tone, 'You know, I don't think I've ever met anyone quite like you before. You have such faith. I reckon you must have been a model student at school – never questioning anything. I agree the Party's doing a good job in moving our country along towards prosperity but they're not perfect – look at all those cases where they've had to expel corrupt officials.'

'But that just shows that the Party recognizes wrong actions when it sees them,' protested Ping, 'it proves my point!'

✦

As he entered his dormitory Wang smiled to himself at Zhao and Ping's response to the internet monitoring. There was a small crowd squeezed into the small dormitory, some playing cards while others looked on. On the top bunk a boy put down his book, seeing his friend's expression.

'Aha, someone's had a good evening – would you care to tell us her name?' he said, grinning.

'It's not what you're thinking. Freshmen girls – man, are they naive!'

The others were intrigued and stopped playing.

'They had no idea that the internet was being monitored!'

'But surely it's public knowledge now. Where are they from – another planet?'

'I wouldn't say it's public knowledge yet, it depends what you read and from where you get your information.'

'Did you tell them about "Jingjing" and "Chacha"?' asked one of the boys at the card table.

'No, they'll find out soon enough.'

Jingjing and Chacha were the names of two cartoon characters adopted by the internet police – the Internet Surveillance Division of the Public Security Bureau – Jingcha being the Mandarin word for policeman. These cartoon characters would appear on the screen whenever 'netizens' – as website users were called – visited sites and forums to remind them not to talk online about anything that they wouldn't talk about in a public place.

'Well, whatever these internet police are doing, there's quite an army of them – my cousin reckons about thirty thousand.'

'Ah, but that's the supposed number of full-time censors and monitors. The provincial and municipal governments are selecting some of their existing staff to do extra monitoring duties. I reckon it's an easy way to increase your pay. Imagine being paid just for reading what's being posted on bulletin boards and putting in some politically correct opinions!'

'Well, I don't like it,' Wang said. 'Why can't we say what we like – where's the harm in that?'

'I suppose . . . ' began another boy, hesitating a fraction as he thought of the words to make his point clear. 'I suppose if everyone is free to post their opinion on a bulletin board then so is the Party – isn't that reasonable?'

'Yeah, but why do they have to spy on us?' objected another.

'Why is it spying?' someone questioned. 'Bulletin boards are like a public newspaper – reading them is not spying. I've read the official explanation of what they're doing: *be proactive in developing discussion, increase control, accentuate the good, avoid the bad, and use internet debate to our advantage.'*

'Exactly,' came the sharp retort. The discussion was getting a little heated. 'They talk about discussion but they are not listening to what people are saying: they're just pushing their own propaganda.'

'I think you underestimate the power of millions of people expressing their opinions – eventually the Party will realize they have to listen and change their views.' The boy from the top bunk spoke calmly, trying to take the tension out of their discussion.

The others decided it would be wiser to leave the argument before they got drawn into saying things they might regret, and returned to the card game

✛

That night as she lay on her bunk, Ping thought about home and about her mother and the neighbours. It felt so far away. But the distance between life there and at university was not simply measured in miles travelled or hours spent on the train. She could think of many other ways demonstrating the gap – spare cash, the styles of clothing, books, entertainment, choice of shops, restaurants, cars. She had even seen a shop advertising western-style toilets! And added to all these things she had discovered another one today – the availability of internet chat rooms. She began to feel almost as though she was in a different country. 'And this university is not even as prestigious as those in cities like Beijing and Shanghai,' she thought. 'What must life be like there?'

Not that everyone in the city was enjoying everything that was available though. She had seen some poor people collecting waste paper and bottles from around the campus. They presumably sold it on to someone else to make a living – but what sort of living was that? She had also seen many beggars, particularly old women and mothers with young children, and badly deformed boys who sat on trolleys on the pavements by the bus stops, waving their tins. She had seen poverty like this in the countryside, but somehow it seemed strange to find it here amidst the affluence. And that wasn't all. Village life was far removed from this place of information and ideas and the open expression of opinions – even to the questioning of authority. She found it strange Zhao had said Ping had faith. Surely everyone has faith in something. Ping's grandmother on her mother's side said people must have faith in God, but she was the only one in the family that said such things. The Party said there was no God! It seemed reasonable to have faith in leaders: if you couldn't trust them, who else was there to trust – yourself? How could you be sure what was best in life – how would you know what to do? Didn't everyone need someone to offer advice and guide them?

From: Jon Perrywell
Sent: November 2004
Subject: November Blues

Hello!

Greetings from chilly China!

If you thought Asia was all mangoes and mosquitoes, you'd be wrong: Shencheng is suddenly beginning to feel wintry (and a bit British). November has been a completely chaotic month. Lots has happened which requires lots of prayers and remembering to keep my eyes on Jesus.

The first rather unfortunate news item is this: I've been ill. The local germs gave me a couple of months' grace period, but they clearly had it in for me and were just waiting for an opportunity to pounce. Which they did, on the last day of October. I was put out of action for nearly two weeks by food poisoning. I had just discovered the dubious pleasures of the college canteen, but alas, I realized too late that stir-fried celery, left lying out until tepid, was not the best. It's times like these I long for suburban boredom and boring British food! I was sick for a day, and recovered, but then a week later I got ill again. By which time it was my birthday, half of which I spent lying in bed feeling like the undead. I managed to have a little party though, and introduced the Chinese to the delights of 'Pass the Parcel'. They were so kind: they came early to help set up and gave me loads of really thoughtful presents which I wasn't expecting. Sometimes the generosity and kindness of local people just blows me away.

I spent the rest of the month trying to recover and sticking to familiar British-style food (fortunately, the Chinese make wonderful bread – it's their best kept secret). I'm now feeling more or less back to normal, but I've got fourteen hours' worth of classes to catch up on, which means the next few weeks are going to be a bit stressful.

The second rather unfortunate news item is this: I have worn a kilt. It was one of the lads' sixty-fifth birthday party, and the other chaps thought it'd be a good idea to make a kilt, as he lived in Glasgow before coming to China. I said, 'great idea', not knowing that the kilts were for us to wear, not him. So, ten minutes before said party, I was presented with what amounted to an immorally short tartan miniskirt, and told to put it on. I spent the evening trying to avoid the cameras and the small children who were wandering around.

In addition, this weekend another bombshell was dropped. SAU, our university, are unwilling to register our training centre for next year. This is where we've been running our English Corner and means that next summer we're going to have to change location. In addition, this February some new teachers are arriving and Shencheng Uni is not going to provide one of them with a visa.

That's the bad news. On to more edifying things . . .

The Bible study group which we were thinking of starting last time round is now well under way. Several people are coming and we've had some good discussions. We're doing a Bible overview, and have got as far as the Law. At English Corner we have had some good conversations too. One girl in particular, Mei, has been challenged by a look at sin, so pray about her particularly and that as we prepare it we will be focused on him and doing it for his glory.

I've been teaching my English-major freshers for over a month now. They are a lovely bunch. Their profile goes something like this: they're from all over the province, mostly very small and female, and mostly aged seventeen to twenty-one. They live in dormitories with communal facilities. They seem to have a lethal work ethic which puts my back-breaking six hours a week at uni to shame. It's great fun to teach them (even if the textbook is archaic to say the least), and they are touchingly appreciative. Pray that God will enable me to point to him in everything I do.

I've started having free speaking time when they come round in small groups to practise their English. Through these times I've been able to get to know them better (difficult when there are 140 of them) and we've had some interesting talks. Most of them come from peasant families and some have family members who are Christian. Their thinking is thoroughly modernist, according to which you can't believe in both God and science: 'Old people believe in God, young people believe in science,' one said to me. 'There is a church in my village but only old and disabled people go,' said another. Please pray for them.

Life for everyone here is about to get very busy indeed. Christmas is coming and we're preparing Christmas parties for our students, culminating in a big bash in a couple of weeks. In all the partying and fun activities we hope to point people to Jesus, the one who was 'born that man no more may die'. Please pray that the Holy Spirit will be working through this and the true good news will get across.

Other news . . .

The weather: mildly cold in the day but bitter at night. Fortunately our central heating has come on, and it is ruthlessly efficient. Again, thanks for your emails, if I haven't replied yet it's because I'm a slacker, and a busy one at that: I'll try to do so soon.

Love to all you good people of Hero Country (that's the direct translation of the Chinese word for Britain, 英国 *Yingguo*

Jon

7.

Mei was in no doubt that today she was thinking and acting differently. It was a pleasing sensation to relate to others in a friendly, caring way and not to allow herself to get irritated by minor inconveniences. Searching her mind for the cause of this new state, the only explanation she could think of was her prayer the night before.

'Hello.' Mei recognized Jon's accented voice.

'Teacher Jon, I have to speak to you,' Mei exclaimed excitedly. 'It's about God. Something's happened.'

✦

Ping soon found herself singing the song that welcomed her and the shoppers crowding into the store, and she swayed from side to side with the beat. Looking round she laughed at the surprise and amusement evident on Zhao's face. Ping knew only a few of the words – 'Jingle bells, jingle bells, jingle all the way . . .' – and made up the rest with a 'la, la, la'. The chirpy tune matched her excitement – she felt as if she were in a palace and gazed around, tilting her head further and further back to look up at floor after floor.

They had taken a bus to the big stores in the city centre. This one was owned by a Taiwanese company which had similar shops in many of the Mainland's major cities. Inside the main glass doors there was a lobby area with a few stalls, coffee bar and drinks machines. Passing through the lobby and pushing through the heavy wide strips of clear plastic (preventing precious heat from escaping) the full magnificence of the place announced itself. An escalator led down to the basement housing the food section, and above them the cylindrical core of the building soared upward to be capped by a huge glass dome. Around the core were six sales floors with escalators leading from one to the other. Ping was awestruck, gaping at the sheer size, the colours, the extravagance – and the people. They milled around her, riding up and down the escalators and peering over the balconies.

Zhao lead the way to the rows of leather coats and jackets on the first floor and tried on a few, under the watchful eye of the nervous sales assistant who was obviously undecided whether she should move these students along or use her sales pitch on them. Zhao was well practised in the art of appearing to be an interested prospective customer, and chatted away to Ping about the merits of each of the coats as she posed in front of a mirror. Ping couldn't believe the prices: three thousand yuan for one coat! How many years would it take her father to earn that? Her eyes glazed over when she thought about her family. There had been no word from her father. Ping was sure he would come home for Spring Festival – now only six weeks away. Zhao tugged on her arm, bringing her back to reality, suggesting they explore the upper floors.

On every floor Christmas decorations were to be found: grinning inflatable Santas welcoming customers as they stepped off the escalators; streamers over and around the areas where products were displayed; small Christmas trees on most sales counters; some staff wearing red hats with white trim and others Rudolf the Red-Nosed Reindeer ones. Though China took pains to preserve its culture and ideology from the taint of outside influences, the Christmas festival was permitted since it provided the people with the one thing they greatly valued – the opportunity to make money and to spend it. So, having thrown out Christianity and its celebrations in the fifties when Communism gave the people a belief system that excluded God, Christmas had been recycled, stripped of its religious content and repackaged.

On one of the levels was a section displaying carvings in wood and jade. There were model Chinese junks complete with sailors, jade dragons, fat Buddhas and a beautifully carved Christmas nativity scene. Ping thought back to the English lesson this week, when Jon had talked about Christmas, explaining that it was part of British heritage. The class had been split into two groups and the members of each group had been given a card that told them which character they were to depict in the Christmas story. They then had to find out how each of them related to the other characters. Ping was a shepherd and needed to find other shepherds and also someone called an angel who would tell them some exciting news and instruct them what to do next. All the talking was of course to be in English. It certainly stretched their vocabulary – angels were new, but seemed to be a bit like the characters in Chinese myths, similar to fairies.

After the students had complied with the instructions on the cards Jon had handed out he asked them to recount the story of that first Christmas. He was evidently pleased they told it more or less in the order in which he had intended and appeared satisfied with the lesson. Ping listened attentively as he then read a piece from a book he said was part of the Bible where the story was taken from, and explained the significance of the birth of Jesus. Ping was puzzled that the apparent purpose of his life was to die. Questions were then invited and someone asked where in the Bible they could read about Father Christmas and how he fitted into the story. Teacher Jon looked as though he would have preferred other questions but launched into some history and traditions that had grown up around Christmas. He encouraged the students to read the Bible for themselves in order to find out more. There were still events and people Ping couldn't fit into the picture. However, history and myths were always a bit like that she told herself: she had never got her head round the sequence of all the dynasties in China's past, or the full story behind the Moon Festival. Jon had suggested that those who wanted to know more about the culture of Christmas might like to come to a Christmas party he was having at his flat. Parties were a favourite pastime so most of the class had turned up. They had played some fun games and sung some songs, some of which mentioned Jesus. Ping had enjoyed herself but still didn't really understand it all.

Back in the dormitory, the girls had discussed the Christmas party and the story Jon had read. Her friend was fixed in her opinion: 'I'm not in favour of Christianity. It's a western institution; it has nothing to do with our China. It's just for old people who can't shake off the myths of religion.'

What the girl said was an ill-disguised repetition of official dogma on the subject, and no doubt subscribed to by her parents. Ping lay on her bed listening to the others' views before deciding what to do. Since the party she had wanted to find out more and had thought about going to church, but the other girls didn't seem to think it was a good idea.

Chun Jiu said 'I'm not interested. Anyway I was planning to spend some time in the internet chat room.'

Ping knew what this meant – she was hoping to have a 'date' with her virtual boyfriend. But Ping wasn't bothered about the chat room and didn't feel averse to the idea of going to the church as her friends apparently did. 'Well, I like new things. I don't see that it can do any harm. It could be fun.'

Having looked on every floor, Ping and Zhao finished shopping and slowly descended the escalators down to the entrance.

'Are you still going to that church next week?' she asked.

Ping nodded. 'Yes, I think I will.'

Zhao shook her head in despair, 'You're a strange one Ping!'

+

'*Jihaode*! Wonderful!' cried Beng's mother, clapping her hands. They stood on the hotel landing gazing down at the scene below.

'Sh, be quiet,' whispered Mr Chu disapprovingly. 'They'll take us for some rustic peasants coming to the city for the first time.'

The hotel had spared no expense in creating a magical Christmas fairyland: an enormous tree, hung with silver chains, little coloured boxes and glittering silver balls reached up to where they stood on the balcony. The manager of the luxury hotel certainly knew his trade and what Beng had thought would be a boring

lunch with his parents now looked rather more prom-
ising.

They walked down the red-carpeted spiral staircase
and were met by the manager who led them to a table
grandly set with an assortment of knives, forks, spoons
and ornate chopsticks resting on ceramic holders. Mr Chu
looked at the wine menu while Beng and his mother surveyed the buffet. A crowd of foreigners flowed down the
stairs from the balcony, so Beng and his mother hastily
filled their plates and returned to their table.

A little girl toddled from the foreigners towards the
Chus' table, and Mrs Chu scooped her up in her arms,
admiring her blonde hair and blue eyes. The girl let out
a wail but unperturbed Mrs Chu simply laughed and
rocked the child soothingly in her arms. The mother
came over to retrieve her daughter and, to Beng's surprise, talked politely to his mother in Chinese, before
returning to her friends.

The restaurant had become quite noisy with the
arrival of the white people but suddenly a strange
silence fell. The Chu family glanced round to see that the
adults had bowed their heads and one of them was
speaking in a low voice. Then, just as suddenly, the
group began chatting again and Beng, looking askance,
saw one of them take hold of what he had assumed to be
a decoration and offer it to another before they pulled it
apart, with the sound of a small firecracker. Objects
spilled out and one was unfolded to become a paper hat.
Soon everybody was wearing one. As Beng looked at the
variety of paper hats, he saw a familiar face staring back
at him.

Jon excused himself and came across to the Chus. Beng
proudly introduced his parents. His mother was over-
joyed and spoke appreciatively to Jon for helping Beng
with his English education. She waited for the foreigner

to respond and realized though he had listened politely, he had not understood most of what she'd said. Mrs Chu turned to her son and asked him to translate. Beng was transfixed, struggling to make an instant translation. His panic and embarrassment grew as the three stared at him, waiting for him to speak. Then suddenly it occurred to him: since his parents knew no English and Teacher Jon knew little Chinese, they would not know whether he was translating accurately or not. Recovering his composure he smiled and made up some kind words to say to his teacher. Everybody was duly impressed.

Wanting to capture the moment, Mr Chu came to life, organizing photos of his son with Jon. Jon called to one of his friends and the final shot was of him and the whole Chu family in front of the ornamental pagoda. Jon then returned to his friends.

'Ha, these are all made in China, as I knew they would be,' Mr Chu pronounced proudly. He had poured the wine and was studying the contents of the crackers. 'According to the latest figures,' he continued, 'we produced over one billion dollars' worth of Christmas decorations, artificial trees, ornaments and gifts. That's 70 per cent of the world's Christmas products – all made in our country.' His father always knew facts like this.

'Just think how clever we are,' he laughed. 'Ten years ago the Party banned Christmas decorations in public places. Now look at all this,' he said, indicating the richly decorated restaurant with a sweep of his hand. 'Perhaps the test of all religion should be – is it good for business?'

From: Jon Perrywell
Sent: January 2005
Subject: Christmas Shenanigans

Alright!

Merry Christmas! (English greeting)

Sheng Dan Kuai Le! (Chinese greeting: Merry Christmas)

Wish you happy every day! (Chinglish greeting)

Happy New Year (and a rather belated Merry Christmas)! As usual, I've got loads of stuff to report back about. December was a very very busy time (and January is turning out to be too), hence my slackness in getting this letter out (sorry again).

Brrrrrrrrrrrr! The Bleak Midwinter hits the Middle Kingdom; for the last three days Shencheng has been clothed in a beautiful white layer of snow. I love it. The last time I was this cold I was sliding down a Swiss mountain. Until Tuesday I had never taught whilst wearing five layers of clothes or ridden a bike through two inches of snow. The latter was especially good fun. Hitting the brakes just turned the bike into a big two-wheeled snowboard, so I had to just use my foot and hope that I wouldn't go into a parallel turn. The roads were full of people dressed in fluorescent orange, who were hacking away at the inch-thick ice covering the surface. Let's say my journey to the supermarket was full of hairy moments – especially when I nearly collided head on with one berk who was cycling on the wrong side of the road (a not uncommon phenomenon).

Well, Christmas in China was fantastic, if a bit mad. I had hoped that by going to China for a year I would escape the usual tacky, commercialized, well-I-wish-it-could-be-Christmas-every-day build-up to the festive season. Oh no no no. China is into Christmas in a big way. It is drinking to the dregs the secularized bathwater of western Capitalistmas whilst overlooking one very important Baby. Tinsel and Santas and flashing lights are everywhere. Even the brothels are decorated . . .

The last few weeks have been ridiculously manic. I have held Christmas parties for each of my fresher classes, cramming thirty or more into our flat. We sang songs and introduced them to Pass the Parcel and the Chocolate Game: they went absolutely wild, like little kids. You don't get parties like that in Britain without the addition of several gallons of alcohol. Some of them brought me presents, small but thoughtful things. My favourite was a Chairman Mao Christmas tree decoration. It was very touching.

Tuesday was a particularly interesting day party-wise: the Chinese celebrate Mid-Winter Day by getting together and making *jiaozi* (pronounced 'jowdzer'), which are dumplings, rather like big tortellini. Some of Simon's students came and we made jiaozi for lunch. One of my fresher classes had asked if they could come round for tea, so they then came and cooked a feast for over thirty people. It was pure chaos but the meal was fantastic, and it was followed by the usual Christmas party carnage. It snowed about two inches that day too – beautiful. It's been so cold that there are still piles of snow lying around today.

So, Christmas Day 2004 was my first white Christmas (that I can remember). It was lovely. We had Christmas dinner at a posh hotel in the centre of Shencheng. It was a buffet and the selection of food was incredible, if rather random; turkey, crab, prawns, oysters, pecan pie, hash browns, ice cream, and even, get this, a selection of breakfast cereals. It was all put out together, starters, mains, and dessert, so choosing what to eat when was a rather gastronomic process. But, my life, it was good. And all for the hideous (for China) price of 88 kuai (about six quid), the price of your average Chinese take-away in Britain.

From there we waddled back to a friend's house where we opened presents, drank mulled wine (Christmas is never complete without it), played games and sang carols. I was worried that I would be lonely at Christmas as this was my first one away from home, but I wasn't at all. Thank you for your kind cards and emails. But most of all, thank God that he keeps his promise (Mark 10:29–30).

Other news in brief:

The end of the semester is imminent, as is Spring Festival (Chinese New Year), which is China's major holiday. Simon, Charlotte and I are hoping to go to Hong Kong and then Thailand. At the moment we're trying to sort everything out (visas, hotels, flights) which is quite a bit of expense and hassle – hopefully it will all be worth it.

I recently got *The Office* DVD box set so Simon and I have been using it to get our fix of British culture. Erm, I think that's about it.

Stuff to give thanks for:

- The group: A new Christian! Pray for Mei, that she grows really fast in her knowledge and love of God.
- Christmas. That loads of people heard about why we celebrate and who it's all about. Also, that I had such a lovely Christmas.

Stuff to pray about:

- My students. I love them to bits. Colossians 4:3–4. That he'll open a door for good things and I'll be bold enough to go through it.

Lots of love and snow down the back of your neck ☺
Jon

8.

It was freezing when Ping made her way to the west gate. She set off along the pavement, carefully avoiding the worst of the protruding paving stones, now pushed out of alignment by cars that used the pavement for parking. She didn't know what to expect and thought of the various temples she had seen. Would there be statues and pictures inside and the smell of joss sticks? After about twenty minutes, she ducked under an archway lit up by coloured bulbs. A sign read 'Welcome to the West Street Three Self Church'.

It came as a disappointment to find a huge bare room – a bit like an oversized classroom. It was very wide with two aisles running its length. Ping assumed there would not be many people here and was surprised by the hundreds of seats – many of them already occupied. From where she stood at the back she noticed that there were a lot of old people, but not all by any means. Ping opted for the middle section and sat down behind a group of old ladies, most of whom were wearing thick padded jackets and woollen scarves to ward off the chill of the unheated building.

A lady dressed in a white robe appeared at the front, and announced the number of a song. Then Ping heard the piano (she was too far back to see it) and soon everyone was singing. There was a movement on her left and song books were passed along the row. She had forgotten the number but checked the book of the lady in front. She soon found her place in the song but it took some time to get accustomed to the tune.

They sang many songs and during the last one some lights were extinguished and she realized there were white-robed people walking along both aisles towards the front. They held song books in one hand and a lighted candle in the other. They assembled in two rows, forming the choir, and continued singing. After that there was a variety of entertainment: more songs by the choir; a short drama involving adults and children; and two boys about her own age with guitars who sang in a lively tempo. Ping clapped enthusiastically and the woman in front turned round and beamed at her with an almost toothless grin saying something in a provincial dialect. Suddenly Ping had a sense of being at home. 'These people are like those in my village: ordinary hard-working people,' she thought. She wondered what the church meant to them. When the clapping died down another woman appeared in front of a high wooden table like a teacher's desk, and read from many parts of the Bible and explained what the words meant. The birth of Jesus came up a lot in what she said and had evidently been predicted many years before it happened. There were also references to his death. Ping listened carefully as she hadn't really grasped what Jon had said about this in English. If only her teacher spoke Chinese.

✛

When Ping returned to the dormitory one of the girls said her mother had telephoned and wanted her to call back. Instantly alarmed, Ping ran to the telephone.

'Wei, hello.'

Ping recognized the voice of the fat, jovial shop-keeper, from whose premises her mother had rung. 'Hello, Lao Sun, this is Ping. Is my mother there?'

There was a delay while Lao Sun fetched Ping's mother from the shop entrance where she'd sat waiting. 'Hello, Xiao Ping, how are you?'

'Mama, what's wrong, why did you call me?' There had to be an emergency, but Ping prayed it would be good news.

'Little Han is not well. Your father's parents are taking him and his brother away to look after them. I may go to stay with them for a short while. I wanted you to know.'

Ping frowned into the telephone. 'Have you told my father?'

'I am trying to get in touch with him but I'm not sure where he is.'

'Ma, I'm coming home. You need me there.' Ping insisted.

'No.' Her mother almost shouted down the phone. Then she spoke more calmly, 'I want you to stay at the university, we must not stop your education, and there is nothing you can do.'

'Oh Ma, Ma,' Ping wept, her large tears falling into the phone's mouthpiece. 'What's wrong with Han?'

'I don't know. He is very weak and can't stand properly. His breathing is bad.'

Ping struggled to control her sobbing. 'Can you give him anything to help?'

'His grandmother is making some special medicine for him.' Her mother's voice sounded hopeless.

'Ma, I have a job here. I'll send you some money for the doctor.'

There was a silence while Mrs Chang considered this information. 'Why are you working? You should be studying.'

Ping replied, 'It's all right Ma, I'm teaching English to a young girl, and it helps me with my own English,' (which was only half the truth since much of the time was spent cajoling the girl away from her toys).

'OK, you're a good girl. Send what you can. Bye bye.'

'Bye Ma, I love you. Tell the boys I love them.' It seemed so ineffectual; surely there was something she could do. Almost without thinking she added, 'I'll . . . I'll pray for you.'

Ping sat on her bed and wept. Zhao came over to her and held her hand. The other girls looked at the floor offering their silent sympathy. Students who did not live close to the university dreaded news like this. They lived in two worlds and were powerless in both.

＋

A chilling wind whipped along the narrow lane leading from the dormitory building to the street and Ping pulled her coat tighter, bending her head lower and clenching her teeth. The wind blew grit and dust into her face but, in her present miserable mood, she was inured against whatever fate or the weather threw at her. She turned the corner and a flurry of leaves skipped around her as she made her way to the post office. Ping had decided to walk rather than take her bicycle, which she would have had to park outside. One never knew when thieves were on the prowl.

Inside the post office there was already a crowd of customers. Perceived social hierarchies defined the order of service rather than time spent waiting, so the end result was a jostling semi-circle around the clerk's booth. Nothing like the orderly line normal in the West, in China those who felt too busy or important to wait simply walked straight to the counter. Asserting oneself was absolutely essential – unless you were prepared to thrust your arm through the metal grille that divided the clerk from the chaos, and wave your document or money before his face, you were unlikely to get served. Calmly the attendant served two or three customers at the same time: totting up the cost of someone's transaction on an abacus (quicker than a calculator); enquiring from another which stamps they wanted; and telling a third they needed to visit the main post office in the city centre. It was an amazing sight and – more amazing still – it worked.

Ping joined the outskirts of the huddle. Coming in behind her was someone in an almighty hurry. He'd stopped his car outside the shop and he obviously considered himself important and his errand imperative. Shouldering Ping aside, he began to push his way towards the counter. Unwilling to relinquish their positions, the other customers braced themselves against his shoves, propelling the man out of the jumble. He staggered for a moment but undeterred, quickly began pushing forward again, shouting abuse at those who refused to budge. As the simmering discontent boiled over the security guard stood up and strode into the crowd. It took some time before his presence convinced the man of his imprudent action, but eventually, denouncing them all as a lot of ignorant peasants, he stormed off.

In the aftermath, the queue reformed, and Ping edged her way forward as the customers shared stories about other pushy people they had encountered. Having arrived in a sombre mood, Ping actually found the distraction entertaining. She concluded ruefully that there were some areas of life where the so-called 'generation gap' did not apply. These people behave just like little children she thought, squabbling over their toys. She herself got to the counter in the end and arranged for twenty yuan to be sent to her mother.

From: Jon Perrywell
Sent: February 2005
Subject: Enter the Rooster

Helloooooo!

And Happy New Year, Chinese this time!

The Spring Festival holidays are over. I've been back in Shencheng about a week, and have had an incredible time since I last wrote to you. There are lots of things to tell you about, but first an urgent prayer request.

One of Simon's friends back home is very ill with cancer and has been told she may only have a few days to live. Her name is Julia, she is about our age and has just got married. It's difficult to know what to pray in the circumstances, but please be lifting up her and her husband to the great Healer and Comforter.

Well.

I'll pick things up where I left off; just after Christmas. And I'll try to not to go on for too long . . .

New Year (i.e. 1 January) was a pretty low-key event. The next three weeks (until the end of term) were spent giving my students oral exams. So last term ended busily. It was also a time of blessing: two girls became Christians. Thank God for them and pray for growth. Also, one of my students, Ping, has shown an interest in looking at the Bible together. Thank God for this answer to prayer. Please pray that we're able to meet up soon and that more people will want to join us. Interestingly, two other students have expressed some kind of interest and both have Christian parents.

In late January everyone in China gets time off for Spring Festival (aka Chinese New Year) and everyone went home to their families around the province: the world's biggest annual migration. Charlotte, Simon and I took the train via Guangzhou and Shenzhen to spend the first part of the holidays in Hong Kong.

How on earth am I to describe Hong Kong? It was an indescribably amazing place and we had a fantastic time. It may now be in the same country as Shencheng but it is worlds, nay, universes, apart. Firstly, the buildings are twice as tall and the streets are half as wide. Secondly, Hong Kong is full of people of every race, in contrast to the virtually mono-ethnic Chinese Shencheng. (You know you've been in the middle of China too long when all the white people you see look the same and you struggle to use a knife and fork.) And after trying to learn Mandarin for six months, coming to Hong Kong where they speak Cantonese (a language which is more staccato and less singy-songy sounding than Mandarin) was a bit disorienting (like learning English for six months and then ending up in Aberystwyth). Lastly, Hong Kong was so much warmer than the Winter Wonderland of Shencheng.

Hong Kong's western-ish-ness (Occidentalism?) and general capitalist degeneracy provided us with a whale of a time. We went to Starbucks, ate fish and chips (with curry sauce, mushy peas and HP, I'll have you know), watched Bolton Wanderers–Oldham Athletic from the comfort of an Irish bar, and enjoyed a quart of Häagen-Dazs on top of Victoria Peak. Simon was staying with his family, so we got to meet them in the lushest ever flat (we even had a man in a purple suit chaperone us in the lift).

We went back to China via Chiang Mai and it was absolutely baking. After a frozen winter in Shencheng it was so nice to be able to crack open the suntan lotion and insect repellent. It was good to have a break. China is not a relaxing place and I was a complete Martha last term (Luke 10:38–42), neglecting to pray or relax, to the detriment of my spiritual life and effectiveness.

Coming back from Thailand was really strange. Going from thirty to zero degrees in four hours is not recommended. After spending ten days in hot, steamy Thailand, we touched down in Shencheng with snow on the ground. I was knackered as we'd got up at 4.30 a.m. for the flight. When I arrived back at my flat relishing the prospect of a nap, I found the locks had been changed. I'd let a friend stay in the flat for a couple of days whilst I was away and the landlord must have thought he was a burglar and switched the locks. I had to spend another hour faffing about and being told to '*deng yixia*' ('wait a moment') before I was able to get in.

After the excitement and delights of Spring Festival, it's back to work in Shencheng now. It was great to return to the classroom and see my students again. The experiences of the new Christians' homecomings were mixed. One girl's sister became a Christian, thank God! But a lad who recently became a Christian got some stick from his parents, and another girl's parents locked her in her room. Please pray for these new Christians, that God will give them strength and their families will be reconciled both to them and God.

This semester I'm teaching sixteen hours a week – four hours more than last semester, so pray that my organization and time management will be good and allow me time to devote myself to prayer (Colossians 4:2). Also that I'll be a good teacher and really be able to help my students. In our first class back, I got them to write a piece describing their spring break. The work they handed in was gut-wrenching stuff. It opened my eyes to the sort of background they're from – stories of which Hardy or Dickens would be proud – of rural poverty, bereavement, separation from parents for years on end (the one child policy means many are sent to live elsewhere when another sibling arrives), hard work on the farm, and hard work at school. My reaction was a peculiar mixture of thankfulness and guilt. It is largely due to me being born in the right place (well, Wolverhampton) and the right time that I've ended up in the ranks of the global rich with loving parents, a good education, and the means to swan around the globe. Most of my students have never left their province (let alone travelled abroad) and have been grafting away all their lives just for the chance to get off the farm. Wow. To whom much has been given, much will be demanded (or something like that).

OK, well, that brings us up to date and I'm really starting to feel the un-comfy seat in this internet cafe. I'm aware that my response to some of your personal emails has been marginally slower than that of a corpse, so please keep harassing me until I get back to you. It didn't help that Captain Braincell here accidentally wiped his inbox in January, leaving no trace of any correspondence.

Right, that really is it, I've got to go and have tea. Happy year of the rooster to you.

Thank you for your prayers and encouragement (Philemon v. 4–7),

Jon

9.

Ping had desperately wanted the first semester to come to an end. She needed to get back to her parents (surely Father would be there) and brothers as quickly as possible. As soon as she had taken the last exam she did not wait for the official end of the semester but went straight to the train station. Others were doing the same, trying to avoid the congestion of thousands of people all going home for the holiday. She queued for two hours for a ticket, then had to stand for three hours in a crowded compartment. She was able to get a bus near to where she lived and walked the rest of the way.

Her mother was digging the ground near the house, her back turned to the path. Ping didn't call out, but put her bags down and studied her mother, trying to judge her health and mood. She certainly seemed as strong as ever, wielding the hoe above her head and bringing it crashing down on the stubborn chunks of earth. But there was a difference in the way she handled the hoe. She was not adjusting her force for the different patches of ground: she was smashing down with equal violence with each swing.

Ping moved closer. 'Hello Mama.'

No reaction.

'Ma, it's me.' She reached out and touched her arm.

Her mother spun round, wild eyed and blinked at her, then dropped the hoe and stood there, her shoulders drooping. 'Ping, it's you.'

Ping spent the first week astutely anticipating the jobs that her mother would want to do and then doing them herself so that they had plenty of unhurried time to sit down and talk. It was obvious that her mother badly needed to vent her emotions. She still hadn't heard from Ping's father, but there was news of a serious accident on a building site in the place where he'd last been. Some of the site workers had died and many were badly injured. She had tried to get news but it was impossible to trace one man among so many, scattered over so many sites. And it was convenient for the construction bosses to fake ignorance of accidents and injuries when there might be issues of compensation or prosecution to consider. She had thought about travelling to find him but did not want to go too far from the two boys, who were still in the care (or was it permanent custody? Ping wondered) of her parents-in-law. Ping and her mother spent a lot of the time hugging and weeping together.

In the afternoon of the eve of Spring Festival they walked to Ping's grandparents' house in the next village as was their custom. When she was younger, Ping had anticipated this day with mounting excitement, asking her mother every morning how many days were left until Chun Jie. When the day finally came, she would run over there in the morning, ahead of her parents, eager to see what grandfather had cooked. Many Chinese men pride themselves on their ability to cook and he insisted on preparing the chicken and tofu dishes which he considered his speciality. Grandmother cooked the vegetable dishes and Ping loved to be around them both and hear them poking fun at each other. Grandfather would look down at her and give her a big wink, then nod towards Grandmother and express his mock irritation at having to share the kitchen with another cook – who only cooks carrots! However, this special place in her grandparents' affection came to an abrupt end when her twin brothers were born.

Ping knew she was second best, even in her parents' eyes. Once, when Ping's father had been working in the local mine, he had been injured in an explosion. The General Office of the State Council had embarked on a major drive to make Chinese mines safer but in spite of some improvements the latest statistics made shameful reading. Although China produced around 40 per cent of the world's coal, it had 80 per cent of the world's deaths in mining accidents. One newspaper report concluded that coal mining had become the most deadly job in China. Fifty men had died in that explosion and Ping's father hadn't been expected to live long.

He had been brought home and she and her mother had taken turns to be at his bedside. He was in a lot of pain and mercifully slipped into unconsciousness much of the time. One day while she was sitting in his bedroom reading her schoolbooks, she heard him call her.

'Xiao Ping, come closer,' he said, his voice barely above a whisper.

She bent over him. 'Yes Baba, can I get you anything?'

He looked exhausted and said nothing for a while but she noticed his eyes were moving, slowly scanning her face, seeming to rest on every detail. 'I have something to tell you,' he said.

Her father never had long conversations with her so she knew this was a significant moment for them both.

'You are a good girl, Xiao Ping,' he began, 'and I am pleased that you are my daughter.'

'Baba, you do not need to say these things – it will tire you,' she said, not wanting him to believe her.

He shook his head slowly from side to side, as if determined to continue before tiredness or pain compelled him to stop. 'I have . . . done . . . some things.' He looked into her eyes for her reaction, but she calmly returned his gaze. 'You had a sister.'

Ping could not mask her surprise and, seeing the look on her face, he turned away.

'We . . . your mother and I . . . did not want her.' She bent closer to catch his words as he was still facing away from her.

'I took her to the mountains.' He slowly met her eyes. 'We wanted a son so badly.'

Ping found herself nodding – was it to let him know she had heard, or that she understood what he had done? Baby girls were not wanted – it was as simple as that. But why was he telling her this – his own daughter?

'A year later your mother gave birth again – to another girl.'

'And I was going to take the baby . . . you . . . to the mountains.' He clenched his teeth to cope with pain – though whether it was the memory or his body that bothered him she could not tell.

'But your grandmother took you from me – to save you. For four years we did not see you and we waited for more children.' He paused and took several breaths. 'But we thought they would never come. So we took you back – and we learned to love you.'

'*Learned to love me.*' His words tore through her. What was it about me that made my own parents have to *learn* to love me? Through her confusion she barely heard his words. 'Then your brothers came and they were everything we wanted. I'm sorry. I'm so sorry.'

Her father had got better and gone back to work in the city, but things had never been the same. Ping knew her parents favoured her brothers, but to be completely unwanted? She turned her father's words over and over in her mind as she and her mother made their way along the stony path to her grandparents' house. Even from a distance Ping could see the door posts traditionally decorated with red paper on which the character for good fortune and happiness – *fu* 福

It had been written upside down. It was supposed to bring good luck, because many years ago, during the Qing dynasty, an illiterate man had inadvertently pasted the character upside down and it had seemed to coincide with his good fortune. Mrs Chang called out as they approached, but instead of the exuberant greeting for which Ping had hoped, her grandparents were quite subdued, offering only polite smiles and formal words of welcome. However Xiao Feng appeared from behind grandfather's legs and cried out 'Mama, Mama!' and the awkward silence was broken. Their mother dropped her parcels, bent down to his height, and wrapped her arms around him, burying her face into the shoulder of his padded jacket. Ping watched her grandparents. Did they have any idea what her mother was going through? It was a long moment before her mother enquired, 'Where is your brother?' Sensing her mood Feng just pointed back into the house, not saying a word.

They soon began their meal and Ping's mother was perhaps a little too fulsome in her praise of the food, taking little morsels over to Han and coaxing him to eat something. Later on they sat around the television and watched the special entertainment prepared by the China Central Television Station (CCTV). Ping wondered if somewhere perhaps her father was watching these same programmes. Silently they sat in the glow of the TV, people measuring their words before they spoke. So much went unsaid between her grandparents and her mother, but she understood the depth of their unease. The boys were too valuable. And now one had fallen ill, they were all looking for someone to blame. And what of the boy's father? Was he even alive? For her grandparents, Han and Feng were their only security. But surely they must see, her mother's loneliness was slowly destroying her.

The downcast group stayed up till midnight, bringing in the New Year with strained promises of happiness and good fortune that none of them truly believed possible.

Writing down these memories of Spring Festival had not helped her state of mind. She had wanted to stay with her mother or try to find out what had happened to her father, but her mother had insisted, at times angrily, that she should go back. They had argued on and off about it throughout the holiday. On her return to the dormitory she said little about it to prevent awkward silences from developing – she knew few people can handle the heartaches of others. She struggled to take an interest in work but doing so was a helpful diversion. Retracing the events in the essay for Teacher Jon simply brought to the surface her suppressed concerns. She searched for words to express her anger at how life had got into such a horrible state. As she finished the assignment, she found it had exhausted her.

From: Jon Perrywell
Sent: March 2005
Subject: Reminded of Reality

Multiple hellos,

The second semester is now in full swing; China certainly doesn't spend this time of year sitting around eating chocolate eggs, and life has been quite busy. Here's the run-down . . .

I have four new classes at Shencheng Agricultural University. One is a rather lively class of 57 forestry students to whom I'm supposed to teach travel English. All good fun. The other three are called 'International College' and I was told to teach them business English. This is a complete joke: I've got no business background except for an AS level and a stint in McDonald's; I may as well be teaching them aerobics. For the textbook, they have given me a big, boring, pirated (it's photocopied) American book on business communication which was blatantly written for native-English-speaking MBA students. I'm becoming gradually convinced that the university don't have a clue about student needs, and neither do they care.

My freshers are as lovely as ever. Over this past week we've been learning about British wedding customs. I made each class do a pretend wedding, which was highly amusing for me and highly embarrassing for them. It's quite funny the way kids seem to grow up more slowly here; they're mostly aged seventeen to twenty, but they're still at the stage (circa age thirteen in the UK) where working with a member of the opposite sex is a fate comparable to eating a bowlful of fresh slugs. In class the boys and girls usually sit apart, and everything seems all very innocent. They were quite shocked when I explained that two of my ex-school-mates now have kids, and that you're allowed to get married at sixteen in Britain (legal marriage age in China is twenty for women and twenty-two for men).

My students also look a lot younger than British teens/twentysomethings. Some of the girls look particularly tiny and emaciated; I suspect this may be something to do with the poor diet of the rural Chinese. It may also be due to the battery farm mentality of the Chinese schools. The education system here treats children as little vessels which need to be crammed full of information at all costs. Middle school is particularly hardcore: a student told me she used to have four classes in the morning, four in the afternoon, and four in the evening. Classes begin at 8 a.m. and end late evening, plus there are weekend classes and homework.

The pressure students are under was brought home rather horribly this week. On Monday morning a student tried to kill herself by jumping off the top of one of the dormitory blocks. She did not die, but, last thing I heard, she was critically ill in hospital. Pray for her and all those affected. One of my lads, Beng, was there when it happened, and told me about it when he came round to practise his English. The girl was on the expensive International College course; apparently her parents were struggling to pay the fees and she wanted to relieve them of the burden. I suspect she may have even been one of the students in my new International College classes. It's difficult to find out details because death is such a taboo here. I've been surprised at my own response to the news; I know I ought to be really upset but I'm not. Has my normally bleeding heart been hardened by the many sad stories you hear in China, or have I been influenced by the extreme reticence of Chinese culture? A bit of both I guess. Or maybe it's because I'm so busy with my own plans that I've stopped caring about others.

A fortnight ago I met up with a couple of my students to do a Bible study together. However, the next week they said they were 'too busy' to meet again. I think they are members of the Communist Youth League. Perhaps they've realized the two don't mix. Please pray that God will open a door for us to start again. On the plus side, the three students from another class came round and we continue to study together: they want to come back next week. Pray God will work in their hearts to draw them to him whilst we study, and that more students will want to come too.

The situation is not so happy regarding the Bible study group Simon had going last semester. Most of them say they're now too busy to meet up. Of those who made commitments last year, only Mei is in regular fellowship. Please pray for the others. Pray that God will nudge them to make time to meet other Christians and give us wisdom about what we can do to help.

For various reasons, including the way the university has treated some of the foreigners this year, the organization that sent me to China has decided not to place teachers here again for five years. It's looking like there'll be no foreign teachers at SAU next semester, let alone Christian ones. God has done some amazing stuff here: there is now a group of about seven Christian students meeting up every week with a local house church leader. Pray that the work God's doing will continue and grow, with or without foreign Christians, and praise the Lord that it is not all about us. I've been inspired by studying Revelation. It has underscored the urgency of what my trip here is about and the need to rely on God 100 per cent.

Another tragic event happened after I'd written the last prayer letter. Simon's friend Julia died. Please pray for her family (especially her widower, who is only in his early twenties) and for Simon.

     Love,

       Jon

10.

Beng looked out the window as the bus rattled through the outskirts of the city. He hadn't spoken to her much, but the girl had sat in the row in front of him in his business class. Many students felt the pressure of expectation from their parents and their own dreams to make something of themselves but Beng had never known anyone to commit suicide. He'd been out on the grass, pacing back and forth as he mulled over the rumours that the university's Party Secretary had committed many misdemeanours. The thud and the shocked silence had snapped him out of his thoughts. He'd spun round to find the girl sprawled on the pathway. And now repellent gossip flew round campus, and he couldn't get the picture of her crumpled body out of his mind. He hadn't been able to concentrate and hoped this class trip to the mountains would provide a pleasant diversion.

The bus had slowed to a crawl behind a truck piled high with straw. The bales wobbled precariously as loose strands tugged free and drifted down onto the bus windscreen. The bus driver jerked out into the opposite lane, seemingly unaware of the oncoming traffic, his choice profanities drowned out by the deafening thump of the truck's large diesel engine. An injury or fatality occurs every minute on China's roads, but the driver seemed little aware of potential carnage. With a few more shouts and a blast of horns, the bus swerved back to the right in front of the truck and they carried on up the mountain road.

Beng's class had chartered the rickety bus especially for the trip. Financial constraints meant the seats were hard, the suspension in need of replacement, and black smoke puffed unhealthily from the exhaust. Despite their private hire, the driver stopped anyway to pick up paying passengers along the side of the road, so before long the bus was overflowing with people and a miscellany of packages.

Rattling on for several hours, the bus finally arrived at the national park and drew up at the ticket barrier. Each student was given a ticket bearing the imprint of three 'chops' (rubber stamps) in the mandatory red ink, and they clambered out and set off up the winding mountain path.

The class walked to the viewpoints, spreading out in small groups. It was strictly a trip for Beng's second-year class but he, as monitor, had 'managed' the numbers and found room for Ping and her friend Zhao. As they climbed up the steep paths the panorama opened up and they grew quiet, awestruck, pointing this way and that at every aspect. There were so many beautiful spots it was difficult to decide which to photograph. They posed alongside flowers, trees and waterfalls, grinning and giving 'Victory' signs. They took a path along a ridge, passing a small temple near a rocky outcrop. It seemed a good place for lunch. Beng and his friends sat down as Ping and Zhao wandered off to look at the temple.

'Did you find the temple interesting?' someone asked as Ping and Zhao came back.

'Yes, we saw some people kneeling down in front of the huge idols, so we did the same and said a prayer.'

'Oh, I didn't know you two believed in God,' the boy replied in a playful, mocking tone.

'Maybe there is a God, maybe not,' Zhao answered breezily, 'but a prayer might bring me good fortune and . . .'

Ping interjected in a more serious tone, 'My family is in trouble and I remembered that I promised my mother that I would pray for them.'

Beng and his friends exchanged grins and shook their heads – their superior male rationality meant they would have nothing to do with such nonsense.

'Teacher Jon prays to the Christian God,' said Zhao, ignoring the boys' ridicule. 'He says his God created everything.'

Beng listened to this exchange with increasing discomfort. This was the talk of old women and uneducated people, and he expected better of his university educated peers. 'Did he show you his God?'

'No, he says he can't.' Zhao explained. 'But he says you can see evidence for a Creator in nature. And that you can see his God changing peoples lives. He said if you seek God with all your heart, you will find him.'

Beng had heard a girl in his senior middle school talk like this. 'If God is so great then he should shout loud so that we can hear him and show himself so that we can see him,' he blurted out, his cheeks beginning to flush.

Another boy spoke up, 'As we know, in China today the people are taught not to believe in the God. No one can prove he exists. We can only believe in science. The teacher in our politics class said that the second basic demand for the building of the Party is: *"adhere to the principle of emancipating the mind and seeking truth from facts"*.'

Silence hung over the group. The other students wandered over, asking when they had to leave. Realizing the time, Beng shepherded the students back to the bus. Nothing more was said on the subject of God.

＋

Mei arrived early and waited at the entrance by the impressive wrought iron gates. The sports ground was a fairly late addition to the university and had been positioned so the back of the arena formed part of the perimeter wall of the campus. There was a suggestion of a cool breeze but yesterday's cold snap had been replaced by bright spring sunshine. Mei, usually very self-confident, was surprised how nervous she felt. But she had seen how glum Wang hd been and realised that his relationship with Lin was behind it. Having offered to help, she had organised to meet Lin and try to find out what the problem was.

She saw Lin in the distance, and raised her hand in greeting. Mei had met Lin a few times before, mostly in the company of others and always felt a little dowdy by comparison. Mei glanced over her own crumpled track suit and scuffed trainers and sighed. She was of similar height to Lin – a few centimetres taller than average – but whereas she was muscular with broad shoulders Lin was slender. She had high cheekbones and almond-shaped eyes, and smiled easily – except today.

'Wang leaves the university next year,' Mei said, once they had exchanged the initial pleasantries.

Lin flinched but said nothing. She knew Mei was acting as a go-between for someone, possibly Wang.

'I expect he will do quite well for himself,' continued Mei. She turned to look at Lin who nodded half-heartedly.

Mei waited, knowing that eventually Lin would feel the tension of the silence and say something.

'Do you have a boyfriend, Mei?' Lin finally asked, trying to turn the conversation away from herself.

'Perhaps,' she offered, 'perhaps not.'

'Exactly,' responded Lin. 'How can you be sure of your own feelings, or of his? Then, how can you be sure he is suitable, and, more importantly, will your parents approve?'

'I know Wang is head over heels about you.'

'And how long will that last?' Lin pursed her lips and stopped walking. She turned to face Mei. 'You must know what it's like to have to respect our parents' wishes,' she said angrily.

Mei nodded. Here apparently was the core problem. 'Tell me about your parents,' Mei said.

'Parent – singular. My mother is dead.'

'I'm sorry. I understand.' Mei responded softly.

'Do you? I doubt it,' said Lin.

'Well, I don't have exactly your experience, but I know of many girls in your position.'

Lin turned and began walking again. Looking straight ahead, she said slowly, 'I doubt if many have a father like mine.'

Mei was puzzled why Lin was taking this so bitterly when she must know many parents still kept to the traditional ways. 'Family ties remain important in our country. Parents want their children to marry into good families. They mean it for the best.'

'Best for whom?' was the acid rejoinder.

'So your father has someone else in mind for you – is that it? – and you don't like his choice.'

'It's not his choice that I resent – it's his method of choosing. I found some newspaper articles in the house that my father had obviously kept.' Mei waited for more and they strolled on further, Lin struggling with her tears. 'They were reports about the recent population census. Do you know the problem that China is facing?'

The only problem of which Mei was aware was China's huge and expanding population – not exactly news and not really earth shattering since it was assumed it would stabilize in a few years. There would be a lot of old people around for a while compared to the number of younger people able to care for them, but this was hardly a problem for Lin.

The report issued a few months ago by the Central Committee and the State Council had made interesting reading. There would be a significant problem in China's future, and one that had seemed to interest Lin's father: gender imbalance. There were more boys than girls and the gap was increasing. In some regions it was said that there were already 130 newborn boys for every 100 girls. Officials from the Population and Family Planning Commission blamed the imbalance on the traditional Chinese preference for boys created by low levels of development, inadequate social security in rural areas and excessive use of ultrasound technology in testing the sex of the unborn.[4] Parents now had the means at their disposal to assist them to get boys instead of girls.

'I think I heard about it,' said Mei, then laughed, 'but look on the bright side – there's more choice for us when it comes to husbands!'

She looked across at Lin, hoping that her comment would help to lighten her serious mood. It didn't, and instead, Lin put her hands on her hips and said, 'Or, in the market place for brides, when demand is up and supply is down, the price goes up!'

Bride price: that was it, Mei realized. Lin was talking about the tradition of paying the bride's family – the logic being the daughter would be lost to her family as she would come under the authority of the husband and his parents, and the money would compensate them for their loss.

'Surely you're not suggesting that your father would sell you off to the highest bidder?' objected Mei.

'My father is a shrewd businessman: I am an asset, and Wang's family is poor. The logic is obvious.'

Mei was appalled at the thought. This was modern China where women are respected as citizens in their own right, not treated as property as they were in the past. She did not want to consider this was still possible but reluctantly admitted to herself that some people probably still acted like this. Surely Lin was mistaken.

'Have you asked your father about this?' she asked.

'Of course not,' was the expected reply. Confronting her father on the matter would be shameful.

'Lin. Your father has invested a lot of money to give you a good education. He does not want you to be like an ignorant uneducated peasant girl who cannot speak for herself. You can surely find a way of discussing issues like this in an objective way without bringing personal issues into it. You must convince him you've a mind of your own and have your own life to live. Who knows, you may be assuming all this about your father, but there may be another explanation.' Mei was surprised at her own heated eloquence and hoped Lin would not become defensive.

Maybe there was another explanation. Lin looked down at the track and pushed some gritty lumps away with her foot. She wanted Mei to be right.

✢

On the way back the rocking of the bus had gradually stilled the chatter and soon many of the students were asleep. In the drowsy hush, Beng shut his eyes and mulled over the day's events. The conversation over lunch had left him agitated and ill at ease but he couldn't quite put his finger on why.

Beng was disgusted by how the university Party Secretary had acted. He was furious he had been so naïve, admiring – no, it was more than that – venerating the man. As the rumours spread about the extent of his degradation, Beng felt an acute shame for being associated with him. For this was yet another occurrence of the endemic malaise eating at the heart of the nation. Bribery and corruption. Some stealing money like this while others struggled on only a few yuan a day? Beng thought of Ping's mother. Ping was reticent in telling him much about her background but he picked up that things were worse than he could imagine. Ping was sending every penny she earned home to help her brother while some greedy party member pilfered money that should have been spent on the greater good, on developing China and making it a nation of which to be proud! And this girl who attempted to commit suicide – rumour said her parents were from a small village east of the city and had sold nearly everything they owned to pay for her university place, and, though no one knew for sure, she had tried to kill herself to relieve them of the burden. How could this be fair?

'How can I feel proud of China's new developments when they're smeared with corruption?' Beng thought.

The park had seemed so beautiful and peaceful: the mellow spring colours; the rugged shapes of the mountain peaks; the cool scented air flowing in his lungs so used to city smog. Beng craned his neck to catch one last glimpse of the retreating peaks, feeling he was leaving one world for another. What if this foreign teacher was right? What if there was a Creator? If I could be so wrong in evaluating people like the Party Secretary, it's not impossible I'm wrong about other things?

Can we only wish for something better? Was everyone corrupt? Where did integrity come from? Teacher Jon obviously thought it came from the Christian God. Was that so ridiculous? Beng put his hands behind his head and sat back against the seat. The Party Secretary had a good record as an honest administrator, everyone had spoken well of him and he worked hard to promote the university in the province. Why had he changed? Beng hadn't really thought about it until now, but even his father kept two sets of business records. Were even his parents corrupt? Is this where it began – in small ways that appeared harmless enough – then grew as one's opportunities and appetites increased?

The bus lurched to the side as a wheel sank deep into a pothole. They were nearing the city and the air streaming past the windows was becoming increasingly thick and grey. As the other students slept, jostled from side to side by the rickety bus, Beng closed his eyes again and let his thoughts drift into sleep.

From: Jon Perrywell
Sent: 15 April 2005
Subject: Day-to-day in a Different Universe

Well, I hope you are all doing well. Time here in Shencheng seems to be flying by. You know what they say about having fun.

Finally feel like I am settling in and am more at home. School has been going well. One of the things that is increasingly striking me about China is how open the place is. There is so much demand for foreigners (English teachers especially) the door is wide open for ex-pat believers to come and share their lives and the gospel with the Chinese. Some Chinese organizations even positively discriminate in favour of Christians (they're less troublesome apparently). I've been challenged to pray for God to send out more workers (Luke 10:2).

Having said that, not an awful lot else has happened on the student front, so I'll use this space to tell you about one of the more amusing aspects of teaching English in China: the English names that students choose for themselves. Some of them choose fairly standard English names (Alice, Kim, Andy). But you also get an assortment of fruity names (Apple, Cherry, Lemon), natural features (Hill, Grass, Bird, Cuckoo), and heavenly objects (Sky, Moon, Sunny). Some names are pinched from the famous (Holmes, Marx, Cinderella), some from the ancients (Athena, Elijah), and some are just plain bizarre (Toshiba, Beyond, Dolphin, Kiwolf). Poor old Simon. He once walked in on a group of students I had round for free-talk time and he asked them to introduce themselves. Their names were Apple, Kathleen, Elfa, Andrea, Lucky, Dragon, Jorpin and Kiwolf. He was struggling by the time it got round to Dragon, he was cracking up at

Jorpin, and when it came for Kiwolf's turn he had completely lost it and was desperately trying to disguise the fact he was doubled up with laughter.

When it came to naming my forestry class, virtually none of them had English names already, so I handed out a list to choose from. I had heavily doctored this list to reflect my general British social circle, and now the class sounds like your typical suburban classroom, complete with Ryan, Lee, Danielle, Kelly, Natasha, Laura and Kev. And most of you dear people now have a Chinese 'name twin' roaming around Shencheng (even you, Dafydd). I'm thinking of making a special Bristol University list but I'm not sure how well the Chinese would take to names like Tarquin or Camilla.

Some bad news though: the large supermarket where I buy all my food has shut down. It closed down without notice and in less than a month all that is left is a rubble-strewn hole surrounded by a nice new white wall. On the wall are now massive hoardings advertising the lush new homes to be built. Things change really quickly like this in Shencheng; you can't get too attached to a place because you know it's likely to be gone in under a year. In this case the reason for the supermarket's demise is that they've built a new and not dissimilar one (it's a chain) ten minutes down the road (alas, ten minutes further for me to cycle).

Anyway, here I'll let you in on the 'Shopping in China' experience. Like many things in China, the supermarkets have been carefully designed to ensure minimum efficiency. Allow me to run you through the procedure of shopping here.

1. Stick your bike outside. There is a nice little enclosure for this purpose and a nice little woman who'll direct you where to park.

2. Go to the cloakroom and exchange your bag for a wristband as you're not allowed bags in the store.

3. Walk past the man guarding the escalator (they're easy to steal, those things . . .). He once had a go at me for taking in my Mandarin phrasebook.

4. Go up escalator to first floor.

5. Walk past the man guarding the stacks of shopping baskets. (Yes, guarding the shopping baskets. Imagine the headlines: Masked raiders make off with shopping basket haul with an estimated street value of $1.2m – Al Qaeda link suspected.)

6. Cross first floor. This contains the clothes, hardware, music and toiletries.

7. Go down another escalator back to the ground floor. There is no direct way through from the ground floor entrance to the ground floor retail space. The escalators are only one-way, so if you forget you needed something on the first floor you need to check out, exit, and go up the first escalator again. Clever.

8. Shop. Here the difficulties properly start. In every aisle there are usually one or more petite young ladies in red T-shirts. When they see you standing there looking dumbly at the shelves, they sidle up, pick the most expensive product off the shelf and try to get you to buy it. If you are not stupid, you will smile and nod before telling them it's too expensive (or, even better, grab what you need quickly and get away before they can strike). If you are stupid, you will try and ask them a question in botched Chinese. They will reply with a rapid flurry of Mandarin, and you will stand there vacantly giving them the dumb foreigner look. By this time other attendants will have

scented foreign blood and be circling round. The original attendant will be trying to aid your understanding by talking louder and faster. You will be flicking through your Mandarin guide (grateful Escalator Man didn't confiscate it) desperately trying to find a word or phrase that could alleviate the situation (politely). By this time you are surrounded by girls in red T-shirts all shouting at you simultaneously in loud, fast Chinese. Flustered, you give them a dumb foreigner smile (which I have perfected), try to leave and hope they don't pursue you. You hope they're not going to think all foreigners are a few cherries short of a gateau.

9. Checkout. Despite the legions of staff loitering around in the aisles, when you reach the tills, all over-staffing problems seem to have miraculously vanished, and it's back to the Sainsbury's-style queues.

10. Get your receipt stamped. After the tills there is a barrier manned by two attendants who will not let you out until you've shown them your receipt and they've stamped it. This is a simple procedure unless you have arms full of shopping bags and your receipt is in your back pocket, in which case you have to do a contortion routine which merely confirms the dumb foreigner image.

11. Get your bag back from the cloakroom.

12. Emerge squinting into the daylight.

13. Give 2 jiao to the bike lady, in return for your bike. (2 jiao: 1.3p. You can't accuse the poor lady of raking it in.)

14. Brave the traffic home.

So there you have it.

Other news . . .

We climbed up a mountain a few weeks back. It was nice to get into the countryside and experience a China which is not all concrete and lead fumes. The scenery was absolutely stunning: imagine Chepstow/Tintern Abbey area crossed with the South of France. (OK, not a good comparison but it's the best I can do after getting up at 6.30 a.m.)

Things on the agenda in the short term: we are heading up to Xi'an for the weekend. It should be a laugh. At the moment we've only got standing tickets for the train, which will make the six-hour journey fun. I'll no doubt have some stories to report.

And a friend is coming over from the UK and we're hopefully going to Tibet together.

Thanks for the support,

Jon

11.

'Let me keep you warm,' said Beng as he put his arm around Ping, drawing her closer. This was the least he could do – what he really wanted was not just to protect her from the bitter chill of the evening but to somehow hold at bay her misfortunes. He felt the touch on his cheek of the expensive warm scarf he had bought her for Christmas and longed to do more for her.

They sat on a concrete bench near the lake in the shadow cast by the streetlight on the willows. Ping had told him about the situation she had found at home at Spring Festival and the anguish she felt at having to leave her mother and brothers. Beng felt angry and frustrated. He wanted someone to be responsible for her distress. The construction boss perhaps, or (though he never dared suggest this to Ping) even a man who abandoned his family because the responsibilities were too great. But the causes seemed too intangible and muddled to sort out. Perhaps it was just fate that was against her? It was so wrong and unfair that families like Ping's should have to struggle on, living such miserable and precarious lives. Beng knew his anger and sense of injustice could do nothing to help. It would not change the people who were corrupt. It would not change Ping's

situation. His anger was simply a vent for his helpless-
ness and frustration, but it made him feel better, almost
as though by getting angry he had somehow con-
tributed to a solution.

What Ping could not see was that, in a very real way,
she was the solution to her family's problems. Ping was
one of millions edging forward to break free from the
tyranny of poverty and Beng got the impression Ping's
mother knew that. He had to encourage Ping to stay at
university so that one day she could begin a career, get a
good job, and from that base help her family and others
like them. He knew Ping wanted to go back to help her
mother but if she did that she would probably sink into
the impoverishment around her, and the cycle would
repeat itself all over again. The government's haste to
enlarge the universities to take in thousands more students now made sense. It was a major constituent of
their policy to speed up development.

Ping felt safe with Beng's arm around her. At the university gates he had seemed such an unlikely friend: he
the son of prospering parents and she the peasant girl. But
she had found a depth in him that continually surprised
her, from which came strength and empathy. It was almost
like one of those traditional fairy tales. But they always
ended 'happily ever after', and she had no such hope.

'Beng, remember that time in the mountains?' she
asked.

'Uh-huh.'

'Remember when Zhao and I went to pray in the temple, and after that we had a discussion about religion?'

'Yes.'

'You never said anything more about it,' she pointed
out, 'do you still feel the same?'

'I don't know for sure. It seems to me there's a huge
gap in our understanding of life. Communism has tried

to come up with all the answers, but it treats us as though we're just thinking machines, trying to make our lives better but with no particular end in view. The sad fact is that I don't think anyone wants to concern themselves about the ultimate end.'

'I don't think I told you about my visit to a church on the evening before Christmas, did I?'

'No, you didn't. What happened?'

She went on, 'Well, I didn't understand it all, but a lot of what the speaker said made sense, provided you accept the notion there's a God in the first place.'

'Exactly,' he agreed, 'I think that's probably where I'm at.'

He frowned in the darkness, trying to analyse his motives for being here. He came wanting to give support and encouragement, but could not suppress his affection for her. He allowed his head to drop, brushed her hair with his lips, and brought his mind back to their discussion . . .

'It seems to me our leaders mean well, and have good ideas for the advancement of everyone, but they haven't got all the answers and they have made many mistakes. If they can be wrong about so many things and if so many in the Party are only trying to benefit themselves without regard for the common people, why should we believe what they say about the existence of God?'

Ping wasn't prepared to go that far in her assessment of the Party's dogma and performance. 'Possibly,' she said guardedly preferring to keep off the subject of politics. She steered the conversation back to a more positive theme. 'Do you remember what Zhao said on the mountain? Something about if you seek God you will find him? Perhaps we should try.'

'How do we seek?' asked Beng, wanting something more tangible as a plan of action.

'Well,' began Ping and laughed. 'Seekers need sign-posts, and we have a choice. We could go to the church I went to at Christmas or speak to Teacher Jon. I think I'd prefer the church, provided we find someone who can answer questions. Jon is very helpful, but his Chinese is not very good and I can't always follow what he says in English.'

✦

The other girls sat on their bunks, listening intently to Mei as she described the things that had happened to her and why she thought God existed. The Bible was the key to knowing about him and that was why they had noticed how much time she was spending reading it. They were fascinated to see Mei so animated about her experience. Her eyes shone with some inner wonder and the girls had not seen her so happy before. They didn't follow everything Mei said, but it was obviously a huge issue for her.

Mei did not find it easy to explain her recent experi-ence – even to herself. The picture that came to mind was of a door that had just opened. Somehow she felt she had known all along the door existed but had just needed someone to show her where it was and how to open it. In answering her prayer that night, God had led her through that door.

It was really quite strange she had not found the door before – but then there had been nobody to suggest that God even existed. What a pity that in spite of all the communist rhetoric and propaganda about the upward march of the people towards Utopia, the key to getting there had been denied – God himself. Mei felt that life would never be the same again because – and this was her breathtaking conclusion as she reviewed all that she had discovered so far from the Bible and the discussions at the group she had been attending – God loved her, specifically her – Mei. In fact love was the key quality in the kingdom of God and therefore she should appreciate love wherever she found it.

✦

'Where shall we sit?' Ping whispered to Beng, peering round the huge room. An elderly lady standing halfway along the aisle waved to attract their attention, and beckoned them forward, but Ping was reluctant to move.

'Come with me.' A male voice came from behind and they turned to see a young man grinning at them, and pointing across to the other side of the church. The student led them to some rows where there were some others their own age.

'My name is Ren Haibin.'

'My name is Beng, and this is Ping. We're students from SAU. Are you a student?'

Ren Haibin nodded. 'Yes, I am in the Science and Engineering University. He turned in his seat and waved to someone behind him. 'There's about six of us who normally come here on Sundays. I'll introduce you afterwards.'

It was a huge relief to Beng to find someone from his own generation here. When he had first walked through the door and seen so many old people it made him recoil, thinking they were making a bad mistake.

'Is this your first time?' Ren Haibin asked.

Ping answered for both of them. 'I came at Christmas but Beng hasn't been before.'

Ren Haibin had a chubby round face and when he grinned as he did now, looking from one to the other, there was a single dimple in his right cheek. Beng had the feeling that he was anticipating the questions that were going through his mind and was probably ready with answers. But Ren Haibin turned his face towards the front and sat back in his seat.

'That's great. I'm glad you've come.'

Ping worried all through the first half hour that Beng was going to be hugely disappointed with the church service and particularly the poor performance of the pianist who accompanied the singing. She was relieved when some of the students were given the opportunity to provide a guitar accompaniment – though she wondered how it compared to Beng's playing. She had asked him to let her hear some of his songs but he had made excuses that they were not that good and maybe he would play to her 'some day'. She half wondered if he was self-conscious about being the rich student with everything he wanted. He hated to talk about things that accentuated the differences between them.

'What do you think of their playing?' she asked.

'They're not bad,' he said, with an approving nod. 'It's a pity they haven't got better instruments to improve the quality of the sound.' He bit his lip and dropped his eyes, and she knew he was regretting criticising those poorer than himself.

After the service Ren Haibin introduced them to his fellow students and suggested they see each other again at the evening service which only the young people attended.

✦

Back in the dormitory, Beng strummed distractedly at his guitar as he mulled over recent events.

So much of life could be encapsulated in that little word 'if'. I have to make assumptions about so many things, he pondered to himself, because, in fact, so few things are certain. A comment his father once made came to mind: 'We are like a mouse who finds himself born in a gigantic *jiaozi* dumpling, and spends all his life eating and exploring but never knowing what's on the outside.' The Party had decided that they knew all the answers to life, which sounded plausible *if* the assumptions and theories could be accepted as fact. But neither socialism, nor the recently arrived capitalism, offered a credible world view, and the government's faith in a mixture of both was purely pragmatic, solving only some immediate problems. This way of thinking lacked an absolute standard outside of itself and therefore the inadequacies of human nature that created it were always bound to corrupt it.

On the other hand, admitted Beng, I cannot prove that God exists, and he remembered what the preacher had said at the church – '*If* I could show you God, he would not be the true God for he would not be greater than our understanding.' It seemed to Beng that whether one followed the Party or God was a matter of choice – or faith – based on reason and experience.

On what he knew and had experienced so far, the God argument won.

From: Jon Perrywell
Sent: 30 April 2005
Subject: Yak to the Future

Evenin' all,

Well, the Merry Month of April hath flown by. My German TV channel has informed me that popes have gone and come in Ye Olde Worlde, a fact conspicuous by its absence from the state-run TV, which, in its daily vomiting forth of sycophantic slurry has remained silent on all matters papal. (Except for one irritated snipe at Italy for granting a visa to the Taiwanese President to mourn the Pope's death. China's still blacklisting him for threatening to declare independence for Taiwan.)

Things are beginning to heat up here in Shencheng. Since my last letter the temperature has shot into the thirties and my cold has turned to hay fever (infinitely preferable as it's usually a symptom of long sunny days). As the term has drawn on, I'm increasingly feeling the temptation to always be doing something. One of the big issues I've had to deal with in China has been the tension between doing stuff for God and spending time with him. I'm such a task-based person that my little head has difficulty comprehending the fact that sometimes Jesus doesn't actually want us to do anything except sit and worship him. So please pray that I'll be able to make time to spend with him without feeling guilty or unproductive.

I've been on another trip up to Xi'an which turned out to be a good laugh. We managed to find seats on the train and ended up in a carriage full of Uyghurs (pronounced 'Wee-gur'). It was interesting to see some for the first time, especially as we'd soon be heading to Xinjiang ourselves. As Uyghurs have their own language we couldn't communicate with them as we shared a mutual incompetence

at Chinese. 'Al salaam a'alaykum' was about as far as
things got. What followed was a generally cool weekend,
spent in a retreat centre surrounded by gorgeous mountains. And I tried fox meat (tough and a bit like pork, but
so smothered in chilli I could have been eating anything!);
I should join the Countryside Alliance. A tiring weekend,
but worth it.

After a few days back in Shencheng, we headed to
Tibet. The following bit requires some explanation. If
you're a foreigner in China and want to go to Tibet you
have to go to Chengdu, a city in Sichuan province, first
to get a permit. From Chengdu you can fly or get the
train into Tibet. The train takes about forty-eight hours
(!), so we flew to Chengdu, got the permit, and flew to
Tibet. At which point the plane turned around mid-air
and flew all the way back to Chengdu. The airport in
Tibet was in a valley and high winds made it dangerous
to land. It actually worked out for the best because in
Chengdu they put us up in a nice hotel and flew us to
Tibet hitch-free the next morning. Better that than getting splattered across the side of a mountain anyway.

On arrival in Tibet we had to stay in Lhasa for a bit to
acclimatize to the altitude. Lhasa is the capital of Tibet.
It's got some nice traditional Tibetan bits, although the
Han Chinese, who have migrated here en masse, seem
intent on turning it into a high-altitude version of
Shencheng (hands up if you love concrete . . .). A large
statue in the centre of town served to remind the
Tibetans that they have been liberated from their previous (presumably concrete-less) feudal existence, are now
marching along the glorious path of socialist development (albeit under some persuasion) and should
flipping well be grateful.

So yeah, an interesting place. We spent a few days
hanging around in Lhasa. There were loads of temples

and monasteries and after a few monastery visits I got completely monk-ed out. There's a limit to the number of Bodhisattva statues and prayer wheels one can see before they all begin to merge into one in your head. The Tibetans are exceedingly devoted people and there were always loads of pilgrims performing circuits, prostrating at the statues, donating money, and burning incense (generally doing everything possible to avoid being reincarnated in Dudley).

After about three days monk-eying round (oh dear, taxi for one!) Lhasa we got a jeep to Nam Tso Lake. The entry pass described Nam Tso as follows:

> 'Namtso' in Tibetan language means Sky Lake. With its altitude of 4718m above sea level, Namtso is not only a salt-water lake with the highest altitude in the world and the head of three big God lakes in Tibet, but also a famous holy land of Tibetan Buddhism.

I describe Nam Tso as follows:

BLUE!!!!!!!!!! It's so blue it would make Margaret Thatcher look red. Seriously. And watching the sun rise over it was mind-blowing/gobsmacking/adjective-defeating. Wow.

We got the jeep back to Lhasa, travelling through massive valleys, past mountains, forests, grasslands, and glaciers. We'd occasionally see Tibetan cowboys on horseback driving along their herds of yak. It seemed to us that a considerable chunk of the Tibetan lifestyle owes itself to this humble animal. Tibetans live in a harsh climate, where often the only other living things in sight are herds of massive hairy beasts: they've ingeniously adapted their way of life to this fact. Clothes are made from yak wool and skin, fuel from yak manure, candles and tea (!) with yak butter, plus yak meat is curried, stir-fried, barbecued, or dried and eaten as a snack as one would eat dried fruit. The downside of this creature's versatility is that in Tibet, most things have a whiff of yak about them. My English friend even swears that the chocolate cake he was eating tasted of yak butter.

Tibet really needs prayer. Firstly, it's one of the poorest provinces in China. Secondly, the Tibetan struggle for independence from China is still rumbling on, with some 'unfavourable' side effects. Thirdly, it's hardcore into its Buddhism. From the little I've read this appears to be all about the accumulation of merit, which will eventually help you to exit the constant painful cycle of death and rebirth (or *'samsara'*). Merit is accumulated by good works, pilgrimages and various rituals (often involving worshipping statues of various Buddhas, gods and departed heroes). It was a bit depressing to see so many people, whose lives were completely devoted to trying to climb up the cosmic order, relying on their own good works to save them. I was actually reading the book of Acts when I was in Tibet and this cheered me up a bit. When Paul arrived in Europe with the gospel, its people had been worshipping idols for thousands of years (e.g. Acts 17:16). But as he preached, people began to respond to God's grace in Jesus, sometimes with pretty disruptive social consequences (e.g. 19:17– 20, 23–41). Pray God will make his gospel spread in Tibet and, like in Ephesus, the name of Jesus will begin to be held in high honour. Pray Tibetans will find freedom economically and spiritually. Thank God for the exciting and fascinating adventure we had there.

Well, we got back to Shencheng and I got on with my latest teaching adventure: teaching freshers using films. The last couple of weeks have seen me using the film *Notting Hill*. This sort of happened by accident due to technical problems (i.e. one ancient computer). I arrived at the university's multimedia classroom only to spend the first 50 minutes of the lesson faffing (or watching other people faff on my behalf) with a Neolithic computer. The long and short of it (or rather, just the long of it) was that I couldn't play all the lovely clips I had lined up and so I just decided to show my freshers a DVD all the way through. I rather stupidly gave them the choice in this matter and as a consequence had to sit through three showings of *Notting Hill* and one of the middle-aged nudity of *Calendar Girls*. The most disturbing thing was that I actually enjoyed *Notting Hill*, all three times, finding it funny and rather cute. Last time I saw it (I was sixteen, it was 1999) I thought it was the second worst film I'd ever seen. What has happened to me? This is turning into a common refrain. Why am I not reading Chomsky, listening to the Manic Street Preachers, and carving anti-capitalist slogans in my flesh, as any well-adjusted politics graduate should? Instead, my downward spiral into nineties man continues. Please pass me my M&S cardigan and the olive oil.

But it has worked out quite well – the students have loved it and I'm trying to milk the theme for educational value – I'm going to get them to act out certain scenes from it after the holidays. It will be interesting to see how they deliver killer Hugh Grant-esque ramblings on the subject of apricots soaked in honey, for example.

I'm still having some good Bible studies with a couple of students. And two of my other students, Beng and Ping, have joined the group the last couple of weeks. Yesterday we looked at the fall, and I felt the group was becoming more open about things. Please pray that the Lord will continue drawing them and bring them to the point of giving their lives to him. One of the Christian girls has said she'll translate for us (which will be a real help) but she hasn't turned up for the past two weeks, so pray she will come next time. And pray for follow-up to last semester's group: everyone seems to be too busy to be interested this semester, even those who said they'd made a commitment.

Election time on our Blessed Plot, I hear. It didn't go too well for the last people who demonstrated in favour of democracy here in China, so you non-expat Brits had better exercise your democratic responsibilities, and do so wisely. If you want a long political diatribe about who to vote for and who not etc., etc., email me back and I will give you one (I'm not holding my breath . . .). But now I will decline to comment except to say this: if a certain party get back in, I'm staying in China. (Alternatively, I could come back and instigate a glorious proletarian uprising to establish the Maoist utopia of the People's Republic of Dudley (The P.R.O.D.). Any takers?)

OK, that's about it. Next week is Labour Day and May Golden Week so another seven-day national holiday. Simon, Charlotte and I are hopefully going to Xinjiang in north-west China, a land of deserts and the Muslim Uyghur people group. It's meant to be an interesting place: the Uyghurs are of Turkish descent. Apparently their food is delicious (hopefully get some kebab action in). So far, no one has booked any plane tickets, so we may end up with a fifty-hour train ride (or cycle). Pray for a good, refreshing trip.

And for those of you concerned about my continuing plummet down the horrific nineties-man abyss, the news is not good, I'm afraid. I've had my colours done. This involved sitting on a chair whilst a lovely lady tried out various coloured fabrics on me to see whether my complexion was best suited to spring, summer, autumn, or winter colours. Not exactly Rage Against the

Machine, I know. Laura flippin' Ashley here I come. At least now I'm looking pretty. Pretty awful, more like.

Thanks again for your support, prayers, and emails. They are very encouraging. I suppose I'd also better take this opportunity to thank you in advance for your patience at all the various ripping yarns I'm going to assail you with when I get back. I've got a few up my sleeve already and I'm sure more will accumulate . . .

Right I'll stop there. Enjoy the spring.

Jon

12.

Wang selected his food at the canteen counter, handed over a meal coupon in payment, then took his tray with its bowls of rice, pork and steamed bread and looked round for a place to sit.

Spotting Mei across the room, Wang slid onto the wooden stool opposite her.

'What are you having?' he asked officiously, unable to hide the irritation in his voice.

'Oh, hi,' she looked up and smiled.

'Um . . . I'm going to try the spicy pork and mushroom.'

'So, what's been occupying your busy life?' he asked, trying to seem casual. All Wang really wanted to know was what Mei had found out about Lin.

'Maybe I'll tell you later, but let me tell you what I think is bothering Lin.' Mei replied, seeing Wang's anxiety for any news.

Wang leaned forward and cupped his chin on his hands, steeling himself for what he feared would not be encouraging information.

'It seems that Lin has got it into her head that her father is more or less going to auction her to the highest bidder,' Mei said.

Wang blinked, frowned and sat back on the stool, his hands gripping the table. He let several seconds pass while he tried to digest what she had said. Slowly and emphatically he responded, 'What the hell does that mean?'

Taking up the cheap wooden chopsticks made from a single piece of wood, Wang broke them apart and rubbed each one against the other to clear them of potential splinters. He picked up a piece of mushroom, and gingerly popped it in his mouth. It was scalding hot and he pushed it around his mouth with his tongue until it was cool enough to swallow.

Mei absently stirred her noodles and studied his face. How could she convey the despair she had found in Lin? Preferring to let her food cool down, Mei recounted her conversation with Lin, stopping several times to answer Wang's questions when he interrupted, astonished at what she told him.

He picked up a mass of pork and sucked it into his mouth. He began speaking, then stopped as he swallowed the mouthful. 'That doesn't make any sense. This is modern China, not the feudal China under the emperors.'

'Strange things still happen, Wang,' she countered, 'underneath all the modern appearance and talk, many people prefer the old ways. Don't you remember the report about that gang involved in kidnapping women and girls and selling them as brides or prostitutes? It's only recently that the government has cracked down on it. But, yes, I agree – I think it's unlikely Mr Yang would involve his own daughter; it's mostly among the peasant classes this happens. I honestly think she's totally misinterpreting the things she has seen and heard.'

'What should I do?' Wang almost pleaded, throwing his hands up in despair.

'She needs a friend,' she said, 'a friend whom she can talk to about it. Perhaps there is something behind all this. She obviously misses her mother and knows she owes a lot to her father for bringing her up. Also he could have been over strict with her as a girl and she is afraid of him. I think she has become rather timid and cowed. Don't push her, Wang – be patient.'

Digesting this was a lot more difficult than the rice. Initially he had wanted to dismiss her report since he just could not comprehend the situation. But Mei was right – Lin sometimes seemed like a beautiful flower struggling to flourish among tall weeds. She allowed herself to be swayed by others and not hold to her own convictions. Was this the result of having a domineering albeit well-meaning father? He suddenly became aware of an intense emotion. He wanted to protect her – stand guard over her. But that is exactly what her father probably felt, and there was a harmful side to that. Lin needed more than that. She needed to be released from obligation and allowed to flourish as an independent person. Could he do that and still restore and maintain their relationship?

Conversation lapsed as Mei and Wang consumed their food. Eating rice from the small bowls required a special technique. Since the surface area of the chopstick was limited the normal method of eating it was to lower one's face to the bowl or raise the bowl to one's lips and with very rapid movement of the chopsticks propel the rice into one's mouth. This was not quite fast enough for some people however, and they had added to this procedure a kind of push-pull system. The bowl was held close to the lips and rice was steadily pushed towards the mouth with the chopsticks. Once the rice got to the edge of the bowl pulling involved slurping and sucking the rice into the mouth. It was extremely noisy.

As Wang propelled the last few grains into his mouth he stared vacantly ahead and saw a student sitting with other boys two tables away get out of his seat. Holding a piece of meat in his chopsticks the student made his way towards a table with a group of girls. Some student prank seemed to be in the making . . .

Wang put down his rice bowl and selected a tooth-pick, covering his mouth with his left hand as he thoughtfully poked at the pieces of pork lodged in his teeth, and craned his neck to see what was happening.

A girl's voice shrieked, 'That's so typical of you – you . . . pig!'

They watched as another girl at the same table picked up a bowl and flung it at the miscreant. The bowl hit him on the side of his head and spilt the remains of pork and gravy down his T-shirt.

Wang watched amused as more voices were raised and other food items were tossed towards the boy and those at his table. One of the boys was hit on the mouth by a bowl from the girls' table and when he wiped his lips and saw blood he became incensed and viciously threw his own bowl back at them. It smashed into the head of one of the girls. A well-built boy, hearing the girl scream in pain, came to her defence and hurled himself headfirst at the bloodied student, sending him sprawling onto the table. That triggered the ensuing riot as other boys took the opportunity to settle old scores.

As a fourth-year student, Wang felt some responsibility to intervene and restore order. He knew no good would come of this, and in his experience everyone present would be deemed to be implicated. He beckoned for someone to join him to separate the fighting boys but they were reluctant, wanting to stay out of trouble, and instinctively made a dash for the door. Wang realized he should not be seen to be a passive onlooker, and with the help of the kitchen staff, began to pull the protagonists off each other. While they held two of them apart, the boy who began the fracas shouted at them, 'There's no place in our China for foreigners who pretend to be Chinese!'

Many of the students were shouting obscenities at each other, but the fight had gone out of them and very quickly it was all over.

'What was that all about?' someone enquired as Wang joined the stream of students leaving the canteen.

'Probably just a lovesick boy who can't take no for an answer and is feeling rejected,' said another pompously.

'No, there's more to it than that,' Mei explained, drawing alongside Wang. 'Did you see what he did?'

'Didn't he just drop some of his supper in her bowl?'

'Not just some of his supper – it was a piece of pork,' Mei explained.

'So – what's so mysterious about that?' asked Wang.

'That girl does not eat pork. She comes from a Hui family. They're Muslim and they have a number of taboos like not eating pork and not drinking wine. What he did was extremely insulting. The Hui normally eat in the *Qingzhen*, the halal place, over the road. That girl must have some important business here that she even came in at all.'

There was a Hui village about fifty kilometres from his own, so Wang knew about the Hui people. The third largest of China's ethnic minorities, the Hui are descended from immigrants to China such as the Arabians and Persians, who arrived in the seventh century. Their foreign origins and cultural otherness lead to the suspicion and jealousy with which Wang often heard his neighbours refer to them. Wang's father spoke about them with evident distaste, accusing them of being troublemakers and spongers and any other abusive words that came to mind. But Wang had never seen any particular evidence for this malevolence. Though they had different celebrations to Wang's village, they seemed to keep pretty much to themselves. That was until last year.

There had been a road accident in the province and a young girl had died. Tragic as it was, it should have been just another fatality due to careless driving or drunkenness. But the little girl was a Hui and the driver was a Han, making all the difference in the world – as far as the Hui village from which the girl came was concerned. Very soon afterwards the driver had been traced to a nearby Han village and the Hui had marched there and demanded that the taxi driver be handed over to them. The headman of the Han village refused, believing the driver would be in safer hands with the police. Thinking this was a ploy to prevent justice being done, a fight ensued with both sides using anything that came to hand – mainly farm implements. The age-old suspicions and distrust came to the fore initially but soon they were fighting for survival, forgetting why it had started. The Hui villagers found themselves at a disadvantage and backed off, but the fighting didn't stop. During the night a request was relayed to other Hui villages to come with reinforcements. By mid-morning the following day, lorries and coaches arrived loaded with men eager for a fight, determined to thrash the Han village. Wisely the Han headman had called the police, convinced that he had not seen the end of the matter and almost at the same time as the Hui mob descended on their enemies, two police cars appeared. Undeterred the angry mob had pushed aside the policemen and started smashing houses and any other property they could find. The police called for reinforcements, but skirmishes took place all through the day and into the night. It made national news until a clampdown was ordered and both villages declared off-limits to reporters. When Wang's father heard the news on the radio about the two villages he almost seemed pleased that his suspicions had been proved right at last. Obviously it wasn't just in the villages that this prejudice flourished. Wang had expected more of his university peers.

✦

'What flavour would you like?' Wang called out, looking into the refrigerated display of ice creams. 'Strawberry or banana?'

'I don't mind – strawberry will be fine,' Lin shouted back from her seat on the park bench.

The park was along the road about a mile from the campus. The site for it had been earmarked in the previous wave of the city's expansion, but it was one of the last places to which the developers had turned their attention. Hence, although it was well laid out with paths meandering round landscaped gardens, ponds, children's play parks, and community areas, it was obviously new. Young three-metre tall trees had been trucked in from the nursery. They had flourished and now offered welcome shade in the summer heat. But to give the park a sense of maturity and history, 'old' tree stumps, carefully moulded from concrete and painted to give the appearance of annual tree rings, had been set up along the path.

Wang paid for the ice creams and with one in each hand walked back through the circle of flowering trees. Lin was looking up to the sky, shielding her eyes from the sun, and he glanced up to see what had attracted her attention. It took a few seconds for him to focus on the kites dancing about in the wind, some hundreds of metres above them. He looked round trying to locate the people who were controlling them. Beyond the trees in an open paved area he could see three men, each holding a simple double-handed winch from which they played out the string.

'What's the date today?' he asked, offering her the ice cream.

'The tenth of April,' she replied. 'Why?'

'The kites reminded me of my home town at this time of year. Around April the fifth when . . . '

'You mean *Qing Ming Jie*, Grave Sweeping Day?' interrupted Lin glumly, still watching the kites, and anticipating what Wang was thinking. The old ritual was still practised but she would rather not be reminded of it.

In ancient times when people were buried instead of cremated, families would visit the graves of their ancestors, remove weeds and sweep away dead leaves. Offerings of food and paper 'spirit money' would be placed on the grave site to ensure that the spirits of the deceased ancestors looked after the family by granting good harvests and the birth of more children. It still happens in the countryside where burials are the normal practice, and Wang himself remembered going to the local burial ground around this time of year. *Qing Ming Jie* also served to acknowledge the cessation of life and its regeneration at springtime.

He caught the sharpness in Lin's response. 'Yes, *Qing Ming Jie*,' he repeated softly, 'how does your father celebrate the day?'

There was a conspicuous delay before she replied. 'He doesn't – not since mother died.' She turned to look at Wang as she licked her ice cream. 'We used to go together to the public cemetery and my father and mother would pay their respects to their parents, though I suspect father never really liked going. He tended to reject traditions like that and especially disliked anything associated with death. So when mother died, we didn't go anymore.'

'Not even to remember your mother?' Wang asked in surprise.

Lin looked away from him at the trees. 'No. I think the memory is too painful for him.'

'What about you, didn't you ask to go?'

Lin didn't answer directly but got up, saying, 'Can we walk around?'

They walked in silence for a while.

'I did ask to visit the cemetery for the first two years after she died but he refused to take me. Eventually I wasn't allowed even to mention the subject.'

Wang stopped and turned to face her. 'You could go without him,' he said, then added 'and I'd come with you, if you would like me to.'

Lin looked at him blankly as though he had said something ridiculous. 'But my father wouldn't want me to.'

Wang struggled to understand her predicament. How could her father have such a hold over her? He deliberately calmed himself and smiled at her instead of blurting out his opinion of her father.

He took her hand in his. 'Lin, he may choose not to remember his wife in the traditional way, that's his decision. But she is your mother and you have the right to remember her as you wish. Don't you think she would have wanted that?'

They walked through the park to a paved area, and stopped to admire the calligraphy artist painting beautifully crafted characters on the cement slabs. He used the long special calligraphy brushes and water. They could still make out two of the characters he had painted earlier, but all the others had evaporated and disappeared.

'It seems such a waste of effort,' Wang murmured.

'It's almost as if he is writing a poem or a prayer that disappears from sight but is still there floating in the air,' Lin suggested.

'That's very philosophical of you, Lin.' He turned his face towards her and shifted to be closer. 'But perhaps the real reason for painting with water on concrete is that he can't afford the paper to practise and perfect his art.' As he said that he playfully and gently pushed her with his shoulder.

She returned his glance and pushed him back, saying with a laugh, 'Or perhaps his wife is fed up with seeing his calligraphy on every wall and won't let him store any more of his work around the house.' Wang studied her as she turned back to watch the artist dip his brush in the bowl of water and begin another character. He loved the sound of her laughter and couldn't remember the last time he'd heard it.

They were both getting cold and decided to leave the park and walk back to the campus. They walked in silence, until Lin turned and said very deliberately: 'I've decided to go to the crematorium next week.' She hesitated for a moment, and then smiling up at him said, 'I'd like you to come with me.'

From: Jon Perrywell
Sent: May 2005
Subject: Going Nuts in May

Good morning from the centre of the universe,*

I feel it's somewhat early in the month to be gracing (?) your in-boxes with my monthly monologue but so much has happened since the last one that if I leave it too long I'll have far too much stuff to cram in – then my already insanely long emails will grow to even more purgatorial lengths.

'Today I've got a special present for you, all the way from Britain . . . ' I told my students yesterday [lots of little eyes light up, 'Oooh!!'], ' . . . the weather!' [groans, 'Uurrrhh']. Yes, the heavens have chucked it down on Shencheng in the past few days. I felt oddly happy: the irritating dust has been washed out of the air and the place feels strangely like home. Unlike in Britain, however, the rain didn't continue for two months solid; we're back to sunshine today.

OK, enough about the weather. The week-long May holiday, which oddly approximates to British May half-term has just gone. As promised we headed to Urumqi, in the province of Xinjiang, China's largest province, up in the north-west corner. It was four hours' flight away, which I spent listening to Charlotte giggling at *The Sacred Diary of Adrian Plass (aged 37 3/4)*.

In Xinjiang we were based in Urumqi, a weird but wonderful Sino-Islamic mix of a city. Now, my time in China has been marked by a series of gob-smacking experiences, but few places have smacked my gob as hard as Xinjiang. One paragraph can't really do it justice, but here goes.

It is a land of deserts, mountains, oil wells, camels and kebabs. A significant portion of Xinjiang's population is comprised of Uyghur people: they are Muslims, speak a Turkish-related language, look like south-eastern Europeans, and eat lamb kebabs, naan breads and other wonderful (but fatty) foods. It's also quite a strategically important area for China, bordered by three nuclear powers (India, Pakistan and Russia) as well as lovely places like Kashmir and Afghanistan. We were staying in the capital city, Urumqi. This is the furthest city from the sea on earth, and it was an amazing place; it was fascinating to see two massive cultures, Chinese and Islamic, Han and Uyghur, side by side in one city. It wasn't exactly Huntingdon's Clash of Civilizations but you could tell things were tense. Han (ethnic Chinese) and Uyghur areas are quite segregated: some parts of Urumqi are indistinguishable from Shencheng whilst others look like somewhere in the Middle East. Having said that, the city had a nice multicultural feel: Uyghurs as well as Kazakhs, Uzbeks, Pakistanis and Russians live there. This was a welcome contrast to the suffocating mono-ethnicity and insularity of Shencheng, where foreigners get stared at like we're from Mars. Urumqi street signs were in both Chinese and Uyghur (which uses Arabic script), and the whole city constantly smelt of barbecued lamb. As hoped, there were plenty of kebabs and lots of curry, pilau and naan bread. Uyghur food is delicious although if I'd eaten it for more than a week I'd probably now be keeled over with cardiac problems. But thank God we were able to have such a wonderful refreshing time.

On our first full day, our little group visited Turpan (the hottest city in China) and went out into the desert where we slept on the sand, under the stars. Next day was breakfast with a Uyghur family, a short donkey ride around Turpan and a return to Urumqi. The day after that we had a day trip to a picturesque place called Heaven Lake. It's as if someone had airlifted a lake and some snowy mountains from Austria or Switzerland and plonked them down in China. It was stunningly beautiful, although I somehow managed to get a cough and sunburn on the same day. We spent the next two days generally pottering around in Urumqi at various places including an Uzbek tea house and a Brazilian restaurant (very very random).

This week it was back to work. Ish. Yesterday I was ill all day and some students brought me round a melon and some apples to wish me well again. Ahh. I'm going to miss them.

I'm enjoying my lessons with my students (especially the freshers) as much as ever, but our time together is drawing painfully short. It's my last set of lessons with them next week. Then I've got to give them exams. ('It is more blessed to give than to receive' is definitely the case where exams are concerned . . .) Please pray for wisdom in wrapping everything up. Particularly pray for a student called Zhao. She wrote me a letter saying she's an atheist and confused by the fact that I said that my happiness was due to my faith in God. I want to write back and 'give an answer . . . for the hope that we have' so pray that I do it 'with gentleness and respect' (1 Peter 3:15) and wisdom.

The Bible study group is continuing. An answer to prayer has been that other students have shown an interest in coming: however, last night none of these other students turned up (in fact only three came). Pray they will come. The studies are (I think) getting more challenging for the group. Yesterday we looked at the prophets and the promise of a Servant who would come and suffer in our place for our sin. Pray that Ping and Beng who heard this will feel convicted and want to accept Jesus as the one who took their punishment. Thank God for a Chinese Christian bloke who came and translated for us. Keep praying for last term's group and wisdom on what to do.

The next few weeks may be a bit busy because I've got to make up some extra lessons for various reasons. I'm also thinking about organising some farewell parties for my students. Pray that I'll still make time for God. My time in China is rapidly slipping away. I've got a month left at SAU, then a bunch of lads are going to come and wreak their own brand of chaos and anarchy on Shencheng for a few weeks under the guise of short-term mission. Then my lovely mum is coming and we'll travel around a bit before heading back to the Shire and you lovely bunch :)

Please also pray for the organization I'm working with. The HQ is lacking personnel and they need people to fill the vacancies here in China. Pray that God will provide the right individuals.

Thanks for your prayers; they are making a tangible difference. God is answering them.

Thing to pray for:

- I will make the most of the short time I have left.
- Zhao – that I will write a clear and honest letter about 'the reason for the hope I have'.
- New staff to fill the vacancies in China once we leave.

Lots of love, especially to you poor creatures undertaking final exams,

Jon

*I know it's not really the actual centre of the universe,** that's just what the emperors used to think.
**The real centre of the universe, as any good astrophysicist will tell you, lies just below Stourbridge bus station.

From: Jon Perrywell
Sent: June 2005
Subject: The Clock Ticks Away

Hello hello hello.

The sands of time are draining away on my time in China; I've only got one month left. My classes at SAU are over as are my students' exams. On the one hand I'm really looking forward to going home; on the other I've never been happier living in China (try and work that out . . . I've given up). It feels very weird.

I'm having to come to terms with leaving my adopted home of Shencheng and all my adorable little freshers. This is turning out to be an emotionally draining experience: I'd underestimated the extent of paternalistic attachment I would feel for my students. I'm going to miss their unquenchable enthusiasm at 8 a.m. classes, their hearty Good Mornings when I start the lessons, their bright eyes, smiles and shy giggles, their cute grammar mistakes and Chinglish, their hunger to learn English, their thoughtfulness and generosity, their child-like innocence, their endless curiosity about foreign things. I want to adopt them all!

To say goodbye, I had a party for each English major class (four in total). They were every bit as chaotic as the Christmas parties, and with equal amounts of carnage, although they were tinged with the sadness of leaving. We played Flap the Fish, the Mummy Game (wrap your mate in loo roll), and the Chocolate Game, always a winner. My parting gift was to teach them the Macarena (ah yes, spreading the cultural sophistication of our beloved island . . . I even have video evidence). In return they again gave me some kind gifts. One girl gave me a leaf. She said, 'I've kept this leaf for many years. The ancient Chinese word for the leaf just means "miss".' That nearly made me crack but for better or worse, my stiff-upper-lipped Englishness prevailed. On a lighter note, one of my students, a very tiny, lovely girl, is called Shadow (see my comments on English names a few months ago). So as a prezzy I gave her a photo of the real Shadow, a beefy man in a sports bra, who only once lost Duel on *Gladiators* (there are probably no a few human beings in the world less like each other).

The end of last week and beginning of this week have been taken up by marking. Marking my freshers' work is always interesting, as it's common for them to pour their guts out to me via their homework (albeit in a restrained Chinese way). The things they write certainly give you insights into their lives and what makes them tick. My other classes' homework was a different story, however. I had to mark 57 guided tours for my Travel English class, the level of enjoyment of which ranked alongside being hit repeatedly over the head with a large cricket bat. Some of them even just copied out chunks from tour guides. They got zero – I'm rapidly turning into a plagiarism fascist.

Meanwhile, Shencheng is now stiflingly hot, touching forty degrees.* The midday weather feels like you've just opened an oven next to your head. This will continue for three months, according to my Chinese teacher. I'm getting a lot of love from Shencheng's six-legged inhabitants, who are anxious to feast nocturnally on this foreign delicacy. Boots' mozzy repellent doesn't seem to have made me any more repulsive (at least not to mozzies . . .).

He gives and takes away, so they say, and just as I'm saying goodbye to my freshers we're preparing for the arrival in Shencheng of some lads from my uni, amongst others. They're going to come and teach English and football to some middle school kids. Next time I write to you it'll probably be in full swing. It's going to be an interesting few weeks. Then Mum is coming on 26 July. I'm going to show her around Shencheng, and we finally leave the great city on 31 July for Beijing. We'll spend a couple of weeks there before going on a package tour of China, ending up in Hong Kong. We finally leave China and fly home a rather convoluted way via Bangkok and Dubai. Touchdown on Our Blessed Plot (Birmingham, to be precise) is 12.20 p.m. on 4 September. Man, that's going to feel sooo strange. (Hey Mum, look at all the funny white people! They all look the same!)

I'm already in a weird enough frame of mind from reading *The Hitchhiker's Guide to the Galaxy*. Sometimes living in China leaves you feeling much like Arthur Dent, confused at the bizarreness of everything and wishing there was something simple and recognizable you could grasp hold of, even just a small packet of cornflakes.

OK, well I've got lots more to tell you about (my mind seems to go blank when confronted with a blank computer screen) but emails are not really a sufficient medium to communicate everything. (My definition of a 'sufficient medium' is a warm summer night and a couple of pints of Banks.) So it will have to wait.

I think the thing that needs the most prayer and thanks is my Bible study group. Your prayers for growth have been answered. Last week ten people came, although there were fewer last night. Another answer to prayer is that two older Christian students have been coming, Hui and Lian. The discussions have felt more open with them around because the other students have felt free to ask questions in Chinese instead of having to always speak English. It's especially good Lian has come. She became a Christian last year and has grown tremendously. She's involved with a local group of Christian students (most of them new Christians). Now the students in the group have a contact with a local group they can go to after I'm gone. It's also good to have her involved as most of my group are girls.

The students have really begun to be challenged by Jesus' message. Last week we talked about his death, and some students came and watched the Jesus video. This week we talked about the resurrection. The end of the study posed the question: if this was true how should we respond? We also watched the end of the Jesus video, which had a brief explanation of how to become a Christian, and a prayer of commitment. There was a long, candid conversation in Chinese between the students and Hui. He asked them if they were ready to give their lives and they in turn asked him loads of questions about what being a Christian was like. Beng and Ping wanted to become Christians (praise God!), Lin didn't appear interested and left, two others wanted to go away and think about it. I told them to write down any questions and bring them next week, and I couldn't gauge the other girl's response. I decided rather than praying and going through what everything meant with Beng and Ping there and then, it'd be wiser to wait until next week when Lian or Hui can take them through things in Chinese to make sure they really understand. Beng had loads of difficult questions about Christianity and Marxism and science – hard enough to answer in English, let alone broken Chinese.

Next week's study is 'What is a Christian?' and it's the last one. Crucial things to pray for next week are:

- The students who didn't come this week will come next week.

- Jesus will continue to challenge people's hearts and those that left this week undecided will want to give their lives.
- Lian will come and be able to lead the girls to Jesus, and ensure they fully understand everything.
- Any new Christians will rapidly get into Lian's fellowship group and quickly grow in faith and knowledge.

This last point highlights a bigger problem. Lots of people have become Christians here through various groups run by Christian foreigners. However, many of us are about to leave and we're trying to set things in place so that the new Christians can grow and continue to evangelize once we've left. Matthew and Sarah, the couple upstairs, are training some new Christian students (three girls and one lad) to lead groups next year. The prospective leaders have matured and are very enthusiastic about the whole thing: they're even learning the guitar so they can worship with music. Pray for Mei, one of my students who is being trained by Matthew and Sarah, for wisdom as she prepares for her new role. Please pray that people who appear to make commitments will get into these groups straight away. Praise God that it's not about us, but about him and his glory.

I've also had the chance to meet up with a couple of Chinese believers. Shen was a good Chinese friend who moved to Beijing a few months ago. He came back for a brief visit so it's been great to see him again. The couple he works for (and lives with) are trying to set up an organization to help equip Chinese believers.

OK, sorry for such a long letter. Other points in brief:

- Five people have become Christians in the group that Simon leads at another university. Thank God, pray for growth, fellowship, etc.
- Some local Christians have been getting some stick from the police. Please pray for security and wisdom. Apparently the government are also keeping a closer eye on foreigners at the moment.
- Three short-term teams are due to arrive in Shencheng. Please pray for safety and practical considerations but also that these teams will have a long-term Kingdom impact here.

Right that's all, folks, for another month. I hope I've been able to convey a little of how faithful our powerful loving Father is, and how he's been answering your prayers. The next email may well be my last unless I can find some way of accessing my account on my travels.

Live long and prosper.

Jon

* Heat wave in Britain? I'll give you a heat wave, you load of wimps . . .

13.

The young Assistant Party Secretary of the Business English Department checked through the list of six names and glanced up, to satisfy himself that they were all assembled here, in his manager's office. He gave a solemn nod to the Party Secretary, who cleared his throat, checked his notes and beamed at them.

'I have asked you to come here today to tell you that you have been granted the immense privilege of joining the Chinese Communist Party.'

It was not real news and the six students waited impassively for further information about the process of becoming members of the largest political party in the world. In spite of its size – around seventy million members – it remained an exclusive club and represented only 5 per cent of the total population of China. The six students comprised three class monitors, Beng among them, plus two students who had shown particular dedication in their studies of the political aspects of the curriculum, and a third who had 'connections'. Hints had been dropped for a few weeks that new recruits were being actively sought: the Party was looking for new blood, partly because some old blood had been spilt, so to speak. An ambitious plan was afoot: to purge the

Party of its corrupt element and to remind all members of their high calling, especially the third of the four basic demands for the building of the Party, *'persist in serving the people wholeheartedly'*. Many members had been expelled for activities that were inconsistent with this demand, including the university Party Secretary. Some of those found to be lacking had been put on trial and a small number had even been executed.

Beng listened to the Party Secretary's speech, and thought of all the speeches he had heard from Party officials in the past. Never before had he listened with such cynicism as he did today. He studied the man, not hearing his spiel but looking for the one ingredient that might have stirred him from his current apathy. Did this man have integrity or was he like all the others? Even the official newspapers had released an estimate that thirty billion dollars a year disappeared from state coffers through the actions of fraudulent officials. Some scholars put the figure many times higher. Beng had heard lots were resigning from membership, though one never knew their motives: did they have things to hide and were getting out before the axe fell, or was it a statement of righteous indignation?

✦

'That's brilliant, Beng,' said Ping excitedly, clapping her hands and skipping round him. 'It's a great honour and you deserve it.'

He laughed at her bubbly enthusiasm, though her reaction wasn't a complete surprise. She became still and looked at him, eyes bright with admiration.

He had told no one else about the offer of Party membership. This was a huge and difficult decision for him and he was almost certain that he would reject the offer,

but he desperately wanted her to understand and hopefully concur with his reasons. It would not be easy: she
had great respect for the nation's leaders and believed
the country was in good hands. He hated to disillusion
her with his own suspicions. Even when he had cited the
arrest of corrupt officials as evidence of endemic corruption, Ping had seen it as an admission by the Party of its
members' wrongdoings and evidence of a desire to
improve.

'I knew you would see it as an honour,' he said, 'and
I love you for your support. But, quite apart from
whether the Party is good or bad, there is a more basic
issue here. Come and sit down.' They had met at the
entrance to a small, enclosed grassy area on campus. The
entrance boasted six white fluted columns between
which were cement seats.

'We said we wanted to seek God, and we have begun,'
Beng said. 'During those evenings in the church and at
Teacher Jon's they told us we have to make a clear decision. Are we going to accept Jesus and his teachings as
being central to our lives, or carry on the way we are –
interested but not committed?' They both knew that
they agreed about the answer to that question and had
begun to understand its implications.

Beng had been surprised at the number of students
who attended the evening meetings in Jon's flat. Some
obviously came along for the chance to get away from
their studies. But most of them came to learn more about
God. One of the foreigners would usually speak about
the Bible and sometimes another student would talk
about how they had come to believe in Jesus, telling of
significant change in their life as well as their struggles.
They had had a time for prayer and it had caught them
by surprise that these people prayed as if God was really
there. It was when they had left Jon's flat after the sixth

of those meetings and were walking back to the campus that Ping voiced her thoughts.

'I think I've decided to become a Christian. How about you?'

He stopped and turned to her. 'I was waiting for you to say that.'

The next Sunday evening they spoke to Jon who took them aside and asked them a few questions and gave them something to read. They prayed and Jon added his own prayer, asking that God would fill them with his Holy Spirit.

Quite a number of the Christians they met on those evenings did not go to the TSPM church, but joined groups elsewhere. When Beng asked about these groups the subject was changed and it became evident they did not want him to know their whereabouts. He asked one of the Chinese Christians about this. 'Where are these other groups of Christians meeting on Sunday mornings? No one seems to want to tell me.'

'Why do you need to know?' he countered.

Beng frowned and said rather crossly: 'Obviously, I don't *need* to know. There're lots of things that I don't *need* to know, but I don't usually encounter such a wall of silence when I ask questions.'

'What they do in the TSPM church building is allowed,' the guy explained, 'because that building is registered with the government department responsible for controlling religious affairs. That means that the leaders of the TSPM church do not have total freedom in leading the church. They are subject to Party control, though this varies from place to place. Other buildings, like people's apartments, are not registered, and any meetings held in them are illegal. It's better not to tell others about them. You never know if you're speaking to a Party informer.'

'I can't believe people take this so seriously,' Beng protested, 'this is modern China – things are changing for the better all the time.'

The student paused, trying to be understanding of Beng's attitude. His own father was a leader in the house church in his town and had been harassed and imprisoned several times. Most Chinese knew nothing of the persecution suffered by many Christians.

'Do you have any idea,' he spoke in bitter tone, 'how many people are arrested each year because they refuse to keep silent about their faith and prefer the freedom to worship and teach about Jesus anywhere they choose?'

Beng had no answer. In a way it did not surprise him that this kind of thing was kept from public knowledge. He felt stupid at being so naïve.

'I want to be committed to Jesus – I really do,' Ping said solemnly. 'But I don't see what that has to do with you being a member of the Party.'

'Well, I think this is the first test,' Beng said bluntly, 'and I'll tell you the reason. You think that the Party's view about God is misguided but since they allow churches to exist, you feel they can't be that bad.' He paused. 'Think about this: how can I join an organization that publicly promotes atheism and seeks to limit and control religious activities?'

'But surely the Party needs good people like you? And you can show them the teachings of Jesus can be good for China,' she insisted.

'Listen to me, Ping,' he said gravely, 'I would not even be allowed to speak about Jesus. That would be regarded as an anti-party activity!'

Ping fell quiet. Finally she said, 'Perhaps I have not wanted to admit these things. You know I hate to criticize any of our leaders. But I think you're right – when we received Jesus and his teachings we said we would try to follow him. We should pray for him to show you what to do.'

✦

The decision made, Mrs Chang pushed herself up from her chair and leaned across the rough wooden table to open the window, normally a source of light or air. But she would not need light or air any more. This act of opening the window had a different purpose – to let her spirit roam free. She did not think of it as an escape because, above everything else, she knew how to endure, how to fight whatever fate threw at her. She knew she was strong – only her strength had kept the little family together, especially when her husband was away for such long periods. But, she told herself, her strength was not needed anymore.

She sat back heavily in the chair, looking through the window but seeing nothing except the pictures in her mind. She saw again the face of the woman who turned to look back in pity as she left the house yesterday – the woman who had brought the news. Her parents-in-law had not come themselves but had sent this woman – this neighbour of theirs – to tell her that Xiao Han had died in the night.

For weeks she had denied Han was getting worse, though the few occasions when she was allowed to see him provided ample evidence – his shrunken face and feeble voice. While he had held on so bravely, she had a reason to live, in spite of being excluded by her in-laws from the lives of both her sons. But now she allowed herself to come to terms with the reality at which her neighbour had hinted: her husband was not coming back; she would not be allowed to bring up her sons; and Ping must be allowed to make her own life, away from all this.

Ping's mother raised her head and looked up to the topmost shelf on the wall beside the door. As she did so, she remembered little Han's voice, 'Mama, what's in the bottle?'

The boys used to watch her lift the bottle carefully down from the shelf and take it outside. She had used it regularly and carefully to prevent her precious crops from being plundered by the pests. It was an effective weapon against every farmer's enemies. Now she would use it to end the daily reminders of the misery that preyed on her, like a rapacious insect, gradually destroying her inner spirit. Han had made his own connection between the bottle and the large vegetables that his mother produced and told his brother that the bottle contained medicine to give the carrots life. She remembered the puzzled expression in their eyes when she gave them a grave look and replied slowly, in a way she hoped would be etched protectively in their memory, 'This bottle contains death.'

From: Jon Perrywell
Sent: July 2005
Subject: Three Lions on the Shirt

Greetings folks,

Firstly a big thing to pray about: my friend Shen. As you may recall he's been working for a couple in Beijing who supposedly help Chinese believers. He started to have doubts about this couple, as to what they were really up to and two weeks ago, suddenly quit his job with them and left Beijing. Apparently things had been getting bad; the couple had become controlling, wanting to know where Shen was, even outside of working hours. On occasions he was even followed by people he didn't recognize. The couple would often be out of the office and he never knew what they were doing except for the fact they had a lot of money (with no explanation as to where it came from). They were very anxious to meet as many Christians, Chinese and foreign, as possible and visit their meetings – they even have offices in cities in other countries with Chinese communities (London, Nicosia, etc.). I've no idea as to whether this is accurate or whether Shen is just being paranoid. Something has definitely spooked him though – he'd always been very calm and mature, but the last time I met him before he left he was nervy and frightened. So yeah, pray that God will be his peace and provision at the moment.

On to cheerier things . . .

Feeling hot, hot, hot? Indeed one is. The men of Shencheng are going around with their shirts rolled up to their armpits and the women with wet flannels on their heads. It's so hot at night that loads of people (including many students) prefer to sleep out on the pavements rather than in rooms without aircon. You can't go out for long without turning into the Abominable Sweat Monster of Shencheng. Special.

The term has now ended at Shencheng University and so has my group. At our last official meeting, we looked at 'What is a Christian?' and at the end Lian prayed a prayer of commitment in Chinese and asked anyone who wanted to become a Christian to repeat it after her. Afterwards I said that if anyone had prayed the prayer, they could come to my flat at 6.30 p.m. on Saturday and I'd run through some things with them (on assurance, faith, etc.) I heard a couple of people in the group repeat Lian's prayer and knew that Beng and Ping said they wanted to be Christians, but the following Saturday no one turned up. I was a bit disappointed at this. Pray that God will continue to draw them to himself after I've gone.

The reason I'd said 6.30 on Saturday was because at 7 p.m. there was a party in Matthew and Sarah's flat, upstairs from ours. This was open to anyone who had ever been to any of our study groups, and its purpose was to introduce them to some other Chinese Christian students and to advertise the groups which will be taking place over the summer, after we've gone. There are two groups happening: firstly, the Chinese Christian students will be running a group on Sunday nights aimed at new Christians. Secondly, another foreign teacher is doing an evangelistic Bible study in her flat aimed at non-Christians. Loads (maybe up to fifty) people came to the party, including six of the students from our group and Hui and Lian. We sang, then about four new Christians gave their testimonies and then we played some games and ate. It was a lovely night. Please pray there will be lasting fruit from this party, that lots of people will feel convicted and many will get involved in groups over the summer. The first meeting of the student Christian group had 21 people turn up: thank God. Also pray for those who have been to groups this year but will not be in Shencheng in the summer, so won't be able to go to the new groups (these include most of my students). Pray that Jesus will prod them to continue to investigate the good news and that he'll bring other Christians into their lives who can witness to them. Many of them have Christian parents which is a real blessing.

All the above seems a long time ago now as the relative calm of the Shencheng summer has been smashed by the arrival of our summer teams. I'm involved with a team of twelve lads from my university Christian Union. They're teaching football in the mornings and English in the afternoons at a local middle school.

It's a real luxury to be surrounded by a bunch of English blokes again (there were only five others in Shencheng this whole year). This is something I've really missed in China: being able to sit and chill out with a bunch of other ineligible bachelors engaging in constructive, manly conversation. Important topics of discussion include: the relative merits of student night at the Bristol Academy (none whatsoever), Third World debt, 1980s and 1990s rock bands (they don't make 'em like that any more), hermeneutics (I had to get that in), and whether Aston Villa are more or less interesting to watch than drying paint. It's also been good fun to see 'China virgins' going through the paces with chopsticks, language tones, and the traffic, just like I was doing a few months back (and still am to certain extent).

The kids they're teaching (11–18s) are wonderful and they learn fast. They've even come to support us in the various matches we've played against local sides. We've taught our adolescent Barmy Army to sing 'Three Lions' and 'Vindaloo', which they do in a rather cute Chinese way ('It is coming home, it is coming home, it is coming, football is coming home . . . ').

God has provided several opportunities for the short-term team already: one of the school teachers (a non-Christian) asked the team to teach the kids about Christ, so they've been doing Bible sketches during their football training. They'll also be teaching their English classes about Christmas and Easter. Give thanks too for the young American Christian guys who were teaching at the school this year, and who have been used by God to prepare the ground so well, and pray that when they return in the autumn they can pick up where we've left off. Pray for unity, health and protection: one of the team had his teeth damaged in a game last week and had to go to hospital, and most of the boys have suffered dodgy stomachs.

There are two other short-term teams happening too: a group have gone to another town in the province to do some teacher training and the other team is teaching English at the college.

Last weekend all three teams went on a trip to Xi'an. The lads arrived in the ancient Chinese capital dressed as if they were about to hit the bars of Faliraki; I even found out yesterday that one of them has St George's Cross shorts. Very patriotic. On the way there and back they insisted on taking advantage of the coach's video to do karaoke to a song called 'Take Me to Your Heart'. This song has been the bane of my existence in Shencheng: it's a cheesy romantic ballad by a Danish band called Michael Learns to Rock. I'd never heard it before I came here, but Chinese people love it and play it all day every day in virtually any shop you care to walk into. Consequently it is branded into my consciousness with a hot iron. Unfortunately the Irish lads

somehow got their hands on a copy and heartily sere-
naded the coach with it (and an assortment of other
Michael Learns to Rock and Backstreet Boys numbers).
On a scale of cheesiness, it felt like death by drowning
in fondue. The Chinese only seem to like the cheese-
encrusted scrapings of the western musical barrel. And
sadly, so do a lot of my fellow foreigners. Where have
all the moshers gone? How I long for some amplified
distortion, loud drums, crowd surfing and sweat. My
angst has been partially assuaged for now by the prov-
idential arrival of a couple of NME and Q magazines.
But what has one year of this done to my musical taste?
At this rate I'll be listening to Radio 2 by the time I get
home (in which case you have permission, nay, a duty,
to have me put down).

The lads brought me up to speed on what is in and out
in the UK. To be frank, I'm glad I've missed the Crazy
Frog phenomenon (and Peter Kay's hit didn't impress
me either when they sang it to me). I hear *Big Brother* is
as tasteful and sophisticated as ever. (*BB* is one thing
from Britain which I definitely definitely do not miss.
Anyway, China has the real thing.) And what's all this
nonsense about banning hoodies? It was odd being here
with the boys and watching events unfold in Britain:
Live 8, G8, the London Olympic bid and the bombs. I
know it sounds strange but Britain seemed so foreign
when I watched it on the telly. It was the first time I've
felt this way: maybe it's time for me to come home . . .

Other highlights of the summer teams being here:

- Meeting a Chinese lady, a teacher at the middle
  school, who has entered the Promised Land. (She
  was on a course at Wolverhampton University last
  summer and actually visited the Black Country
  museum.)

- Nearly convincing an innocent American girl that the British call eggs 'thumbledoodles' (or TDs for short).
- Meeting a taxi driver whose only English was 'Long live the People's Republic of China! Long live the Chinese Communist Party!' and a memorized dialogue: 'How do you do? My name's Hu. Where's your sister? She's in the countryside.'
- Winning our final football match on penalties (It was 1–1 at full time).

The short-term teams are leaving within the next few days and so are some of the beloved people with whom I've been spending my year. A weird kind of grief is setting in: I'm going to leave Shencheng in two weeks' time after spending over ten months in the city. I'm finding this hard to deal with, especially as things have been so rushed recently and I've had little quality time to wind things up with people. It feels strange and sad. I guess when you choose to do a year like this, harrowing goodbyes are an occupational hazard. I think the most important thing for me now is 'closure' (horrible word, I know) and to spend some time with the people I've been closest to all year: Simon, Charlotte and Joyce. But they are all heading off to Tibet very soon, so I'm worried that I'm not going to get an opportunity to be with them. So please pray that Jesus will help and provide for me, and that in all the changes he will be 'the strength of my heart and my portion for ever' (Psalm 73:18).

Lots of students have now gone home and the campus is back to the way I found it last August: hot, calm, and alive with the comfortingly familiar sound of students practising musical instruments.

This is probably the last email you'll get from me in China, although I may send a kind of post-match commentary from the comfort of the UK, so can I just say thank you so much for supporting me: it's been a fantastic blessed year and I've seen and felt the difference your prayers have made. Hopefully I'll get the chance to thank you all individually when I get back (not long now).

OK, well that's all folks. When I get back to Britain I may be a bit odd (well, more so than usual), so I apologize in advance (the technical term is 'reverse culture shock'). I also apologize for anything (Uncle Albertesque) I say beginning with 'When I was in China . . .'. Buy me a chocolate milkshake and I'll shut up.

Love and Peace,

Jon

14.

'But love is the greatest thing of all. The Bible says so.'

Lian listened with frustration as Mei expounded her philosophy.

'I love him and he loves me. Love is a gift from God.'

'And what about Mr Luo's wife and child?' Lian asked with a level tone.

'If there is no love in the marriage, the partners must seek love elsewhere,' Mei answered bluntly.

'There is more than one kind of love, Mei. You are simply thinking of the romantic kind. There is love for a parent or a child, love for God, even love for the truth and what is right.'

'Yes, I agree. I love God, and the truth and my parents.' Mei replied brusquely.

'Mei, please think about what I am saying. God instructs us through the Bible that wives and husbands are to be faithful to each other. A sexual relationship outside of marriage is sin.'

'But sex is part of love so how can it be a sin? Why did God give us bodies and these feelings if we are not to enjoy them with a man?' Mei was never one to mince her words.

Taking on the student Bible study group after the foreigners had left, Lian now felt out of her depth in handling this situation with Mei. Lian despaired of getting through to her, when the girl obviously did not want to listen. Mei seemed intent on moving in with Mr Luo – perhaps she had already.

Lian decided to battle on. 'It seems to me, Mei, that you have been very selective in your reading of the Bible. God has given us sex as a gift but he has also warned us about its misuse. Think about other gifts: food, for instance. He has given us food, but he also warns against gluttony.'

'Yes, I agree,' retorted Mei. 'I intend to be faithful to Mr Luo. It would be wrong to sleep around with lots of men.'

'Mei, you told me once that your parents had an arranged marriage. Do you remember?'

Mei nodded.

'But your father has been faithful to your mother ever since?

Mei saw where Lian was leading and said, 'There is no love in their marriage; I think I told you that too.'

Lian pressed on: 'What would you have felt if, when you were very young, your father had abandoned you and your mother and gone off with another woman?'

For once, Mei did not have a ready answer. The truth was, though there seemed to Mei to be no love between her parents, her father had been like a rock. A cold, hard rock most of the time but totally dependable and protective.

'I don't know,' was her weak reply.

'I think you do, but you do not want to see yourself as that girl running off with a married man, and possibly destroying the life of Mr Luo's wife and child,' Lian said sharply.

Mei was silent for a long time. Lian prayed inwardly for a change in her.

'I can't help it. I can't stop seeing him.' Mei had lost her confident tone and she stared at the floor.

Lian sensed the struggle going through her, and longed to be able to do something but felt helpless. 'The Lord Jesus can give you strength, Mei, but not if you resist his will.'

Mei looked up at Lian, tears forming in her eyes, and shook her head. 'I'm sorry,' she choked out the words, 'I can't help it.'

The moment had come that Lian had been dreading. Mei was a natural leader and Lian was worried about her influence on others in the Bible study group.

In recent weeks there had been a number of students who had asked Lian and Hui about Christianity and the Bible. One boy, for instance, had shown her a book that his Chinese teacher had been using in their culture lessons. It contained large extracts from the Bible, and the student obviously knew of the study group and asked openly if they could help him understand more about it. So Lian had invited him and others to the Tuesday evening study that continued to run in Joyce's flat. She gave them an overview of the Bible showing them the various threads that ran through it from the Old to the New Testaments. Though most of them struggled with the very idea of God, they seemed prepared to put the issue aside for the moment. Their young minds were not slow to appreciate the historicity of the people and events and eventually to grasp the implication of the life and death of Jesus. Mei had been invaluable in helping Lian and Joyce out when the students' English was insufficient to grasp what Joyce, the foreigner, was saying. It was clear the students admired Mei and listened carefully to her explanations.

'I'm afraid I must ask you not to help with the Tuesday evening study group any more,' said Lian. 'I believe what you are doing is wrong and you would be setting a bad example to the others.'

+

'You should reconsider your decision.' The Party Secretary was sitting behind his huge leather-covered desk. He smiled condescendingly at Beng who stood in front of him and continued, 'I have offered you a wonderful opportunity to advance yourself.'

'I have thought long and hard about this,' Beng replied. 'I do not want to become a Party member – at this time.' He felt it wiser not to give his reasons. After what the other Christian had said about informers and secrecy, he decided he did not want to implicate any of his friends by speaking of his real reasons for not becoming a member. By adding 'at this time' he thought he could convince the Party Secretary that there was still hope. Indeed, he told himself, if the Party changed its constitution and erased atheism as one of its central tenets, it might be possible for him to reconsider his decision.

'Beng, perhaps you are mixing with people who are leading you into bad ways?' The Party Secretary made it his business to know everything about the students and teachers. He knew those who had religious and anti-party sympathies. While they were few and kept their opinions to themselves he was content to ignore them. By giving these individuals a certain amount of freedom they sometimes led to the bigger fish who were propagating such dangerous nonsense. So far Beng had done nothing illegal, but the Party Secretary hated to see bright students with so much potential become poisoned with false and outmoded ideas. He needed Beng to admit to his recent interest in religion, and where it had come from.

'I would never do anything against my country,' asserted Beng, avoiding the trap.

The man realized that he was not going to get any further, gritted his teeth and rose from his chair. 'Then you give me no choice. There will be consequences. You may go.'

✢

The statistics published by the Suicide Research and Prevention Centre in Beijing indicate that nearly three hundred thousand people commit suicide every year in China. Many of these people are young rural women who use the painful but effective method of drinking pesticide.

The news of her mother's suicide was sent, thankfully, by the wise village headman to the university office, so that Ping did not have to open the letter among her chattering dormitory friends, but in the director's own office. And the director had the foresight to call in Ping's friend Zhao as well, knowing how close the two girls were.

It seemed to Zhao there is no good time to hear bad news. It either comes when life is good and pleasurable so it makes you feel guilty you were enjoying yourself when others were miserable or in pain. Or, it will be yet one more thing to add to your pile of woes. It had been only a few days before the dreadful news of her mother had arrived that Zhao had told Ping the bad news about Beng.

Zhao had been sitting in the canteen one morning, having come early to avoid the breakfast queues. Immersed in her own thoughts, she was suddenly conscious of a large figure beside her. The massive fleshy round face of Yin Hong grinned down at her. Yin Hong was rude and arrogant, a typical 'little emperor', spoilt by his parents who were both members of the Communist Party. His arrogance won him few friends and he got by on his connections alone.

'Mind if I join you?' he asked, not really bothered if she minded or not, seating his heavy bulk rather too close to her, and putting down his bowl of rice.

'I'm in a hurry actually,' she replied edging herself away a little. Though Yin Hong was not in her college year, she knew of his reputation.

Yin Hong was quite used to being cold-shouldered. Apart from his usual cronies, most students, girls particularly, soon found urgent things to do when he came near. He was fully aware of the hidden sneers but did not often get the opportunity, as he now had, to respond in kind. 'I've just had some good news, and wanted to share it with somebody,' he said.

She glanced around the canteen. There were quite a few others sitting at the tables – why did she merit his attention? 'So, what news is this?' she asked, trying to be polite.

'Well, it seems that your friend Ping has got herself attached to someone who's out of favour,' he said, before filling his mouth with rice.

Zhao reacted as he obviously intended. She put her chopsticks down and turned to face him. 'What do you mean? And why is this good news?' she exclaimed.

He deliberately ate slowly to maximize her anxiety. 'Well, it seems Beng has done something to annoy the Party Secretary and is no longer the class monitor,' he said finally, clearly pleased to be able to make this news public, 'and guess who's been chosen to be the new one!'

From: Jon Perrywell
Sent: August 2005
Subject: Conclusion: Those Caterpillars Were
Fast As Lightning

Dear all,

Thought I would give you an update. Even though I have left Shencheng, so much has happened. We have been in Beijing and it has been a completely different experience – lots of food for thought.

My last week in Shencheng was pretty hard. The short-term lads left on the Sunday and a lot of the other Shencheng-ites went off to Tibet. I was totally gutted I couldn't join them, but the holiday plans I'd made were set in stone so we had to say our goodbyes.

After more or less everyone had left, Mum arrived and she was really sick for the first few days which compounded the gloom I was already feeling about leaving. But she recovered and we got the flight to Beijing to begin our Chinese mini-odyssey.

I left Shencheng on 31 July. After spending so much time there it was strange to be in Beijing. After a year in Real China, we hit Tourist China – a weird and wonderful parallel universe. Visiting Tiananmen Square with its legions of police and riot vans at the ready brought it home that, for all the KFCs and David Beckham posters, China's government is still a communist dictatorship which tolerates little dissent and idolizes Mao, a man whose policies led to the death of around fifty million people.[6] (That's about the same as the number of soldier and civilian deaths during the Second World War and more than the number killed by Nazi genocide.)

Beijing is like Shencheng only really really really really big. I was surprised how similar the two cities were as I thought they would be worlds apart: Beijing too has the communist concrete punctuated by glittering skyscrapers, the phalanxes of bicycles (nine million – they were right, I've counted), the chug-chugging blue Dongfeng trucks, the gorgeous food, the piped music and the pervasive smell (a combination of cigarette smoke, car fumes, boiled noodles and raw sewage). The significant difference here is you get none of the stares and 'HELLOOOO!'s which I was subjected to in Shencheng because Beijing is crawling with foreigners. Hundreds of 'em.

One night there we walked through a little walled hutong community on the edge of the city, where most of the migrant workers live and it just reminded me how bizarre China is . . . In shiny Wudaokou, a sector of Beijing full of cash, skyscrapers, loaded foreigners, and overheated property prices (complete with Starbucks, McDonald's, KFC and Pizza Hut) is what is basically a slum, with narrow mud alleys, corrugated iron roofs, and no proper sanitation, inhabited by the people who build the skyscrapers. One tube stop, two universes.

There is quite a cultural diversity that wasn't found in Shencheng. South Koreans are identifiable by their attire, which is rather more bling than the conservatively dressed Chinese. Von Dutch beanies, funky hair and massive headphones is the preferred look. I've heard there are even some North Koreans around: apparently they wear suits, are accompanied by government minders and aren't allowed to talk to anyone except each other and the Chinese. I've yet to see any, which is a bit of a shame (George Bush's 'Axis of Evil' holds a certain appeal).

I had the privilege of watching the spectacle of a South Korean football match from a local beer garden. Korean fans are very different from English fans: most of them are small, shrill, and female. If one of their players touches the ball (not all that common an occurrence, it has to be said), they scream like a bunch of twelve-year-olds about to meet Take That. There must have been hundreds of Korean fans there but I found it a lot less intimidating than if they had all been English (in which case there'd have been no glass left in Wudaokou, save for that spread across the pavement or embedded in people's faces). Still, the squealing red horde was enough to bring out scores of riot police, and by midnight they had the whole thing shut down. I think it was H.L. Mencken who said that puritanism is 'the haunting fear that someone somewhere may be happy'.

This week we also ventured outside the city. We took a road trip to Northern Hebei province near the Inner Mongolian border, with a view to riding some horses. Now I know I'm an ex-Bristolian but this was not the Tarquin-and-Camilla-type of horse riding. There were no helmets, and the second horse I tried to ride had gallop as his default setting. Rather than summarize the experience, I will give you a few words and phrases and you can fill in the blanks: chafe-age; extreme pain; sudden ability to reach James Blunt's higher register. Glad I did it though. Galloping across North China, I felt like Genghis Khan (or one of his eunuchs, anyway).

The best thing about the place was the air: after being in Beijing where the level of pollution equates to a twenty-a-day smoking habit, breathing in the cool clean air was the most glorious experience.

Next we travelled by boat down the Li River to Yangshuo which for me was the highlight of the summer. Yangshuo is a tiny little town in south-west China, surrounded by the gorgeous scenery you see in paintings in Chinese restaurants. It was a complete backpackers' paradise, awash with Lonely Planet geeks, fake T-shirts and chilled-out cafés and bars. Seriously, if ever any of you decide to do the whole Asia backpack thing, you can't miss this place.

Another interesting place was Shanghai. It's China's biggest city but for some reason sort of reminded me of Liverpool. Mum and I went up this ginormous building called Jinmao Tower. The guidebook (which I swear by) told us that you could either go up to the observation deck on the eighty-eighth floor or for the same price go and have a coffee at the bar on the eighty-seventh. So we arrived on the eighty-seventh after traipsing around for seeming epochs. We entered a swish bar: the lighting was atmospheric, the music chilled drum'n'bass. The staff stopped me and said there was a dress code and I would have to change my three-quarter-length trousers for a pair of theirs. Unfortunately the pair they gave me had no fastener so I had to walk around with my hand on my waist to stop them falling down. The irony was that the bar was full of other scruffy student backpacker types who'd obviously read the same paragraph in the guide-book. Mum and I eventually ended up having a meal there against the backdrop of amazing views of Shanghai (and it cost less than a meal at a pub in Britain).

But on the way back to the hotel we were reminded of the other China as we went through a subway. There was a girl about seven years old sitting begging. Her face was disfigured and parts of her hair were missing. I gave her a pack of peanuts I'd nicked off the plane but Mum had to go back and open them for her because her hands were little more than stumps with maybe two limp fingers hanging off. She looked as if she'd been severely burnt. It was a sad sight, and I felt powerless to do anything about it. So when people tell you about how impressively fast China's economy is growing, spare a thought and lots of prayers for those, like that little girl, who have been left behind.

Well, that's nearly it. We are off to Hong Kong tomor-row. It's been good to see a different side of life in China

– this time the rich/student/metropolitan/ex-pat side of things.

God bless,
Jon

15.

The phone rang in the sitting room and Beng ran through to answer it. His father got there first. After a brief conversation, Beng was handed the phone. 'It's Ping,' his father said with a knowing smile.

'Have you heard about the foreign teachers?' Beng detected anxiety in Ping's voice.

'No, what's happened?' he asked.

'They're not coming back next year. The university won't issue them any contracts!' Ping said, sounding indignant.

'How do you know this? Have they given a reason?' Even as he asked the question Beng realized what the answer might be.

'No one knows for sure, but some say it's because they didn't keep the terms of the contract. It may be something to do with the group.' Ping sounded puzzled.

'I think I can guess what's behind this, but let's not discuss it on the phone. We'll talk about it tomorrow,' he said and put the phone down, now somewhat more discrete in telephone conversations than in the past.

'Is there a problem? Ping didn't sound her usual cheerful self,' asked his father, standing in the doorway.

'She's upset about what's happened to the foreign teachers. They're not coming back.' Beng replied.

'Oh, that's strange – I thought you had a high opinion of them.'

'They are good teachers – but they have introduced us to . . . ' Beng hesitated, 'other ideas.'

'Ah.' His father nodded sagaciously. 'So they've fallen out with the Party Secretary.'

There were times when Beng realized there were many hidden depths to his father. Mr Chu obviously knew a lot more than he ever spoke about. He had probably summed up the situation with the foreign teachers perfectly accurately.

'Yes, probably,' agreed Beng, looking glum. No doubt the Party Secretary knew the source from which Christianity had recently spread and had forced the Foreign Affairs Department to end the foreigners' contracts. The dean had hinted to Beng that he had made enemies by not joining the party and should be careful from now on.

'Beng,' his father spoke kindly to lift his son's spirits, 'let me tell you something.' He came into the room and sat down facing his son. 'This country is changing – fast.' He dropped his voice. 'The Party is a dinosaur that risks sinking under the weight of its bureaucracy and dogma into the morass of corruption it has created. In your lifetime and possibly even in mine, there will be a new government. Already, in Beijing and other cities, the Party is totally discredited, and the thousands of protests around the country will force changes through. Fortunately there are a number of enlightened people in government who may be able to ensure that the changes are peaceful.'

'I see,' said Beng and lots of questions sprang into his mind – by whom, when and how would this come about. But he knew his father would not speak about the details and, frankly, he didn't need to know.

'Anyway, Ping is OK, is she?' Mr Chu saw that his son was not going to draw him into politics, so changed the subject. Mr Chu had met Ping only once but knew immediately what had attracted his son to her – even though she was a peasant girl. But he had reasoned that with the disappearance of her father and the death of her mother, Ping was now released from her ancestry. Fate had broken Ping free from her roots in the muddy soil. She could make a good wife for his son one day.

'Yes, she's fine now,' said Beng, 'after we went to her mother's funeral and she saw her brother was being looked after well, her grief began to heal.'

'And is she able to look after herself?'

Beng knew what lay behind the question. After Ping's mother had died there was great debate about whether she would be able to support herself and stay on at the university. Ping continued the part-time teaching job, but insisted on sending her pay to her grandparents to help with the upkeep of her brother. In pity for Ping's situation, Zhao had initiated a collection for Ping, and approached students individually including Beng himself. Somehow the word spread and some teachers even made contributions. Beng's father had also got wind of it and, realizing her predicament, had given generously. Zhao had told Beng about his father's donation after making him promise that he must never tell Mr Chu he knew. It was a side of his father Beng had not expected to find and he felt indebted.

'Yes father,' he said, 'I understand that some people have been very generous.'

✦

The familiar landscape sped past. Twice a year for the last four years, Wang had travelled this route to spend spring and summer holidays with his parents. But now school was over this would be Wang's last trip home for a long time. Lots of things seemed to be coming to an end: lessons; exams; dormitory life; campus basketball. Wistfully Wang thought back to the closing moments of his last – and best – game.

At the centre circle the referee tossed the ball and the centre player tapped it back to the point guard. He dribbled the ball up the court, weaving around the opposing centre and forwards then passed it across to Wang who was just outside the three-point goal line.

'Shoot, Wang!' Lin cried out. 'Now!'

He sprang and thrust the ball over the guards and watched it drop into the net.

'Goal!' The crowd roared with delight as Wang got his ninth basket and twenty-first point. Seconds later the referee blew his whistle for final time. They had won, thanks to his last shot. Lin waved excitedly from the side and he ran across to her.

Staring out of the window of the speeding train heading further and further south, away from the university, Wang enjoyed the memories of the four years there. There had been many times when he would have gladly given up and escaped the restricted life, but he recalled the poignancy of the graduation ceremony and the leaving parties during which the students had to face being wrenched away from familiar landmarks and close friends. Many of the boys found the embarrassment of their tears quite difficult to handle. Now he was going home for a short break before heading off to work in the development zones like thousands others. His prospective employer was a joint venture between China and Germany, producing fertilizers and animal feeds. He would join the marketing department.

The score of that last game was great, but it was a secondary matter. What mattered was that she was there, cheering him on. An animated, vibrant Lin, who grinned and joked with him.

'Only nine baskets today, Wang,' she laughed, and flashed her eyes at him. 'You must be getting distracted by someone.' She handed him a towel to mop his face, as he squatted down to get his breath.

When he had recovered he stood up and kissed her cheek.

In the row behind were Mei and Mr Luo. Mei waved cheerily. Wang knew he had been right in concluding that Mr Luo, though married, had feelings towards Mei, and by the look of things Mei had welcomed his advances. Was this where the wave of religious fervour that had swept through the campus had taken Mei? In Beng's case he had become righteous, refused to join the party (this had never been given as the official reason, but rumours normally have some truth in them) and had lost his position as class monitor. Neither outcome seemed particularly satisfactory if that was all Christianity had to offer.

Wang leaned forward, took another handful of sunflower seeds from the packet on the table and sat back in his uncomfortable seat, thinking about Lin. Never before had there been anyone in his life like Lin to encourage or inspire him. Back home, life was too busy and exhausting for parents to get excited about much else beyond the size of the latest crop of carrots. Sports and hobbies were peripheral matters. Even his academic results were not praised but compared with those of someone else who had done better, with unspoken disparagement. Forced to look outside the family, he had found some measure of inspiration in the success of Chinese athletes like Yao Ming, China's best basketball player, now playing in the American leagues. However, that level of success was out of his reach – literally – since at 2.29 metres, he towered above Wang's 1.82 metres. But now Wang wanted to do his best for Lin and she seemed to be able to unlock in him energy and ability he didn't know was there. And not just for sport. He had found a new drive for his studies, even though he longed to spend more time with her. He realized that he had left it rather late in the day to get a place among the top students, but he had wanted to do more than coast along and just scrape through the exam. He had pushed himself hard in those last few weeks and managed to score 81 per cent.

The train cleaner interrupted his reflections as she waited for him to lift his legs before sweeping her mop quickly over the floor and hurrying to the next cubicle. The ticket collector came in. Wearing a smart, military-style uniform, he was accompanied by two other similarly dressed officials and all three checked Wang's ticket. Why three men were needed Wang did not know. He had long ago given up making sense of officialdom. Perhaps this was an attempt to protect the state railway from dishonest officials. The drinks cart came by and he waved the steward on, pointing to his bottle of water on the table. Another steward came along behind, selling items from a tray hanging round his neck.

As the carriage became quiet again, Wang returned to his thoughts. Distance could be a problem. He had no idea how often he would be able to get back to see Lin, but phone calls were cheap. He had not wanted to go so far, but there were few jobs in the city that interested him: in fact she had told him not to settle for just any job, but to be selective. That had seemed a luxury at the time – most of the students became desperate and were prepared to take anything that gave them a salary. But Lin cautioned him not to take the easy option, and eventually he came across a company that appreciated his farming background and marketing qualifications. His fluency in English seemed to have impressed them at the interview and clinched the job. Looking back, he still couldn't believe his good fortune in finding a girl like Lin. He had heard lots of new ideas about love these last months on campus, especially the love of God. Mei spoke at length about it but the person that Wang found most convincing was Beng. His beliefs were so strong. He had even incurred the wrath of the Party Secretary rather than change his mind.

The train slowed down and glided into a station, and soon more passengers came through to his carriage, among them a foreigner who sat across the aisle from him. Wang studied the man wondering where he was from. He stood out from the other passengers in so many ways: his choice of clothes, casual and coloured, compared to the black or brown clothes of the Chinese; and he had blond hair. An elderly Chinese man began to engage the foreigner in conversation, asking him where he was from. Grinning nervously, the foreigner nodded, obviously not understanding a word. The old man then proclaimed to the surrounding passengers that this was another ignorant foreigner who could not speak Mandarin, and proceeded to verbally bully him, asking the foreigner why he had come to China if he wasn't prepared to learn the language. One or two of the passengers took pity on the foreigner and smiled kindly at him, but the others, glad of the distraction from the boredom of the journey began to speak of their own experiences with foreign tourists. Wang decided to go to his rescue.

'The man wanted to know which country you come from,' he said.

The relief on the man's face at hearing his native language was immense.

'That's so kind of you to translate for me,' the foreigner said, in an accent Wang recognized from some English language tapes and films. 'I appreciate it. Actually, I am from the United States of America, from the state of South Carolina.'

The other passengers were awestruck at Wang's ability to speak in the foreigner's tongue and the carriage fell silent. From then on he became the official translator. After a while, conversation gradually lapsed, some of them slept and the foreigner took out a book to read. Wang felt the train slowing down again as they approached another station. His thoughts returned to Lin and her father. He had not believed it possible he would ever meet him face to face. But Lin had prepared the way. She told him that after their visit to the cemetery where the remains of her mother were held, she had gone home that weekend and told her father what she had done. He had been sitting in their apartment reading the newspaper at the time and Lin said he slowly put down the paper and stared at her in a curious way. Moments passed and Lin steeled herself for his outburst. But all he said was 'Good' and resumed reading. And that seemed to be the beginning of a new relationship.

Following Lin's announcement that she had gone to the crematorium, and thereby asserted herself for the first time, she began to take a hand in her father's domestic life. The apartment was quite dowdy and unwelcoming: its décor was virtually the same as it had been at the time her mother died. Essential repairs had been done, but it clearly lacked a woman's touch. Lin began in a small way to bring colour and beauty into each of the rooms. Pictures, table coverings, curtains and lighting were changed so that the whole place began to look entirely different. She insisted on replacing the lazy cleaning woman who had obviously taken advantage of a man who cared little for his surrounding. Her father appreciated the changes and encouraged Lin to totally redecorate and even allowed her to choose new furniture. All this took some weeks as she was only able to get back home at the weekends, but the result was amazing – and not just to the apartment. Mr Yang became more talkative, and went out more to meet old friends. It was as though the transformation in his home corresponded with one in his soul. Lin decided that it was time she should introduce Wang, and invited him home to meet her father. She would have cooked, but her father insisted on cooking, as he had done when his wife was alive. There was minimal conversation and Mr Yang busied himself in the kitchen, then focused on eating, and afterwards watched television. However there were many moments when Wang knew he was being closely studied.

Lin told him that after he had left Mr Yang had said to her, 'My daughter, you have shown me that you make good choices.' As he spoke he pointed to all the changes in the apartment. 'I hope you have made a good choice in Xiao Wang.' And that was all he said to affirm Lin's relationship with him.

The train was nearing Wang's destination when his mobile buzzed and he saw a text message from Lin: 'Good luck, I'm always thinking of you.' Wang snapped the phone shut and strode through the carriage, throwing open the train door as if to his future.

From: Jon Perrywell
Sent: September 2005
Subject: Conclusion Part Deux!

Alright!

A big hello from the Midlands. I'm sitting here among these dark satanic mills, safe and sound wondering what on earth happened to the year. It is, as I expected, very weird being back on my soggy little island. But more of that later (this email is a beast, I'll warn you now). I'll resume the narrative from where I left off. I just thought I'd send you a final update on how the summer's been and how the situations I described in the last email turned out.

Our time in China ended in Hong Kong, where the weather was ridiculously wet. (That's what being an ex-British colony does to your climate.) Talk about raining cats and dogs, this was raining elephants, giraffes, hippopotamuses (hippopotami?) and many other large animals. I spent my last evening in China appreciating the refined culture of this ancient and sophisticated civilization by, err, going to Murphy's Irish bar to watch Aston Villa play Manchester United. The less said about the result the better; let's just say that my love for Man U is not exactly flowing like milk and honey down Aaron's beard (to mix biblical metaphors horribly).

After a quick stopover in a gridlocked Bangkok (my year has been Thai'd at both ends, so to speak) and a few hours in Dubai airport we landed at Birmingham.

What was the first thing I did on getting home? Well of course, I instilled a revolutionary consciousness in Dudley's proletariat, enabling them to break their chains of ideological slavery and emancipate themselves from the hegemonic thought patterns induced by global capitalism. Working together as comrades, we engaged in class warfare and expropriated the local bourgeoisie, sending them to Bromsgrove for re-education before razing to the ground that cradle of capitalist filth that was the Merry Hill Centre. And behold, the red flag was unfurled over Dudley Castle. And lo, the counter-revolutionaries and reactionaries were fed to the sea lions at Dudley Zoo, never to exploit the masses again. Thus was our land liberated to bathe in the red glow of the dawn of a new Utopia: long live the P.R.O.D. (People's Republic of Dudley)!

Erm . . . actually, I went to the pub.

So what of Britain? It's a very strange place. Why is it strange?

1. Rain.
2. Cold.
3. No Chinese people. Well, there are a few. But I had to stare through the window of the Four Seasons in Wall Heath to get a glimpse of a real Chinese person. The woman behind the counter must have thought I was mad (she would not have been the first).
4. Carpets.
5. People look miserable. (An unfairly generalized observation due to the fact I made it at the baggage carousel at Birmingham airport. Baggage carousels are generally miserable places.)
6. Eerily quiet. Where are the jackhammers, the newspaper sellers, the chanting communists? (Wolverhampton?)
7. The smell. Not raw sewage, dust, sweat and two-stroke engines but a gentle breeze bringing the scent of pine woodland, flowers, creosote and suburban lawns.
8. When I overhear a conversation in the street I can actually understand it. (The other side of the coin is

that people can understand me so I have to watch
what I say . . .)
9. Deodorant.
10. When you go in a shop, assistants don't follow you
around.

So, dear reader, I will probably see you some time in the
near future. But let me get two things straight first.

1. Please don't ask me to order a takeaway for you in
Chinese. The reason being most people in Britain
who run Chinese takeaways speak Cantonese,
whereas I've been learning Mandarin. You might as
well go to an Italian restaurant and order in French.
2. The question 'How was China?' is as broad as
[insert something that's very very broad] (my
vocab fails me) so please maybe try to be a little bit
more specific. Otherwise you may get a load of
incoherent verbal vomit as I attempt to describe the
indescribable. But so you're pre-briefed (is that a
word? Am I talking Chinglish?), I'll try and sum up
my experiences here.

To say this year has been mind blowing is an under-
statement. China is not a place to go to relax: it constantly assaults your eyes, ears, nostrils, taste buds,
pride, preconceptions and prejudices. Looking back, my
first few weeks in Shencheng were insane. Coming from
the cosy British suburbs, it was like landing in a parallel
universe. Every culture has an invisible rulebook of the
way things are done and I think it's only when you go
somewhere different that you find out what's in it. Here
are some examples. In winter, my students would open
all the classroom windows and shiver through the lesson in their thick coats. Why? Because you need fresh

air. In April, with soaring temperatures, they're still in their thermal underwear (don't worry, I never checked this out). Why? Because the weather's changeable and it's easy to get a cold. If you go to the dentist, they'll operate on you in the window of their shop. Why? Because then everyone else can see if they do something wrong, so you feel safer.

Even so, it's hard to generalize because China is such a huge place, and it's also full of contradictions. A socialist country with less welfare provision than 'capitalist' Britain. An insular culture which is opening up to the world. A country which invented so many things long ago but today lags behind the developed world in its technology. A country where people can be so officially unfriendly and bureaucratic but personally so welcoming and warm. A place where people are so enthusiastic about learning but where the government censors the media in case they learn too much. And a place where people are now enjoying more freedom and wealth than in the past five thousand years but where the government still refuses to treat them like responsible grownups. Trying to work through these issues has mangled my head a bit, on top of the fact that by the end of the year I was still rendered largely deaf, dumb and illiterate by the language barrier. I'm amazingly grateful to the many lovely Chinese people who would go out of their way to help me and make me feel welcome.

I've had some updates from the people back in Shencheng so will let you know how all those situations turned out . . .

The student group is continuing. Twenty one people came to the first meeting, a major answer to prayer; although I think numbers have levelled off since then. On one Sunday the meeting lasted for seven hours! On that occasion a homosexual joined the group. He said he'd accepted God in his heart but still wanted to look for a boyfriend. Pray that the Holy Spirit will lovingly convict him to give his entire life to God. The leader of the group has now left Shencheng for a job in the south of China, so it's being led by the students, most of whom have been Christians for less than a year. One of the leaders, Ping, recently sent me an email: 'Our meeting went very well in this holiday. We led to study Bible one by one. We started from Matthew, and we finished 6 chapters. Because this week is first week [at university after the holidays] for some people, we'll have a meeting this Sunday night [4 September]. I am trying to tell everyone about this thing. I hope many people can come.'

Please pray for Ping and Beng as they lead the group: that God will give them wisdom beyond their years. Pray that God will use the group to bring lots of students to Christ. Pray also that he'll protect them from security threats.

Hui, the student who helped translating in Simon's Bible study group is facing opposition for his faith. He was due to visit South Africa and France later this year on business for the company he's just joined. He's never been out of province so he was excited. But his manager was indulging in some dishonest business practices. He was concerned about this, so he confronted the manager about it. The manager got angry and cancelled Hui's overseas trips. Praise God that Hui had the confidence to stand up for his Christian values. Pray God will give him the strength to continue to do that, and pray his witness will draw his manager and other colleagues to Christ.

This term there are, as far as I know, no Christian foreign teachers at SAU. Pray for the students there, that they will still be reached by the gospel, either through the students' study group or by some other means. My ex-students have got a new English teacher though, a Canadian called George. They told me he's into astrology, conspiracy theories and the like (although they don't believe the stuff he says). Pray that God will protect them from this.

Shencheng seems to have changed so much since I left. Apparently they have started to build wealthy suburbs on the outskirts of the city. These suburbs are expanding at a ridiculous pace: rows of tacky Butlins-esque flats have been joined by massive quasi-European apartment complexes and large American-style wood-clad detached houses, complete with gardens, high gates and even gas-guzzling people carriers and four-by-fours. It really is a breathtakingly dynamic place (especially compared to places like Oxford where any building newer than eight hundred years old is considered a little too trendy and modern). Having said all that, comparing Shencheng to Beijing has made me realize how undeveloped Shencheng is.

OK, I really do think that's all folks.

I also got back just in time to head down to Soul Survivor in Shepton Mallet. I was there with OMF (they were the ones who put me in touch with the organization I worked with in China), running a stand to try to persuade people to think about serving God in East Asia. Pray that God will use this opportunity to mobilize workers. The fields are white and all that (it really is true).

Seriously, thank you for putting up with my extended random burblings for a year and thank you for sending me some very nice emails back. I have appreciated them.

Throughout this year it's been amazing to know that you've been interceding for me. So again, thank you very much for taking the time to think and pray about his work in China: I really am grateful and thankful to

God that he's given me such wonderful praying friends.

May the word of Christ dwell in you richly (Colossians 3:16).

HAPPY EVERY DAY!

Jon ☺

Endnotes

1   See: Tim Luard, 'China rethinks peasant "apartheid"'. BBC News, 10/11/05. Available: http://news.bbc.co.uk/1/hi/world/asia-specific/4424994.stm. See also Fei-Ling Wang, *Organizing Through Division and Exclusion: China's Hukou System* (Stanford: Stanford University Press, 2005).

2   Stephanie Hemelryck Donald and Robert Benewick, *The State of China Atlas* (Berkeley, CA: University of California Press, 2005).

3   Hello (plural).

4   It is now illegal under Chinese law to use ultrasound for the selective abortion of female foetuses. For further information see http//www.telegraph.co.uk/news/main.jhtml?xml=news/2005/01/09/wchina09.xml&sSheet=/news/2005/01/09/ixworld.html.

5   The Chinese government has in fact instituted democratic elections but only at village level – the bottom of the political pecking order. The rest of the political system retains its authoritarian characteristics.

6   Historians' estimates of the number that died under Mao range from twenty to seventy million. A summary of sources can be found at http://users.erols.com/mwhite28/warstat1.htm#Mao.

English-Speaking OMF Centres

Australia: PO Box 849, Epping, NSW 1710
Tel: 02 9868 4777
Email: au@omf.net
www.au.omf.org

Canada: 5155 Spectrum Way, Building 21, Mississauga,
ONT, L4W 5A1
Toll free: 1 888 657 8010
Email: omfcanada@omf.ca
www.ca.omf.org

Hong Kong: PO Box 70505, Kowloon Central PO,
Hong Kong
Tel: 852 2398 1823
Email: hk@omf.net
www.omf.org.hk

Malaysia: 3A Jalan Nipah, off Jalan Ampang, 55000,
Kuala Lumpur
Tel: 603 4257 4263
Email: my@omf.net
www.omf.org.my

New Zealand: PO Box 10159, Dominion Road,
Balmoral, Auckland, 1030
Tel: 09 630 5778
Email: omfnz@omf.net
www.nz.omf.org

Philippines: QCCPO Box 1997-1159,
1100 Quezon City, M.M.
Tel: 632 951 0782
Email: ph-hc@omf.net
www.omf.org.ph

Singapore: 2 Cluny Road, Singapore 259570
Tel: 65 6475 4592
Email: sno@omf.net
www.sg.omf.org

UK: Station Approach, Borough Green, Sevenoaks,
Kent TN15 8BG
Tel: 01732 887299
Email: omf@omf.org.uk
www.omf.org.uk

USA: 10 West Dry Creek Circle, Littleton,
CO 80120-4413
Toll free: 1 800 422 5330
Email: omfus@omf.org
www.omf.org/us

OMF International Headquarters: 2 Cluny Road,
Singapore 259570
Tel: 65 6319 4550
Email: ihq@omf.net
www.omf.org